I0211404

Early Quakers and Islam

Early Quakers and Islam

Slavery, Apocalyptic and Christian-Muslim Encounters
in the Seventeenth Century

Justin J. Meggitt

WIPF & STOCK · Eugene, Oregon

Studies on Inter-Religious Relations 59

To the memory of Melanie Jane Wright (1970–2011).
Bless ástin mín.

Wipf and Stock Publishers
199 W 8th Ave, Suite 3
Eugene, OR 97401

Early Quakers and Islam
Slavery, Apocalyptic and Christian-Muslim
Encounters in the Seventeenth Century
By Meggitt, Justin J.
Copyright©2013 by Meggitt, Justin J.
ISBN 13: 978-1-4982-9194-1
Publication date 2/16/2016
Previously published by Swedish Science Press, 2013

Contents

1. Introduction

Reviews of early modern European receptions of Islam are, quite rightly, legion,[1] and there are useful, if somewhat variable, treatments of the subject in broader surveys of Islam and Europe, the West, or Christianity (the terms often treated, somewhat problematically, as synonymous).[2] There are also helpful analyses of early modern European constructions of the Ottomans and their empire,[3] a focus that is somewhat narrower but which would have made sense to many Europeans of the time: although Europeans were conscious of distinctions between, for example, the Islam of the Maghreb, Levant, the East Indies, of the Mughals[4] and the Safavids,[5] in most European languages the term 'Turk' normally subsumed them all – as Ahmad bin Qasim, a Morisco, complained on his journey through France and the Low Countries on behalf of the Moroccan emperor in the early seventeenth century.[6] However, this essay's

---

1   See, for example, Blanks and Frassetto 1999; Tolan, Laurens and Veinstein (2012); Haug-Moritz et al. 2010; Hertel and Schuelting 2012; Heyberger et al. 2009; Höfert 2003; Klein and Platow 2008.
2   Cardini 2001; Dakhlia and Vincent 2011; Goddard 2000; Hourani 1992; Konrad 2011; Lewis 1982; Reeves 2003; Rodinson 2002; Watt 1991. Given that one third of Ottoman territory and its capital lay within the continent of Europe, 'Europe' is not a useful term to use in this context, particularly for the early modern period. Early modern 'Europeans' tended to think in terms of Christendom. See, for example, Claes Rålamb, the Swedish ambassador to the Sublime Porte in 1657–1658, who described crossing the Danube at Silistra in Wallachia in 1657 as setting his foot ' out of Christendom into Turkey' (Rolamb [sic] 1732: 679).
3   Bisaha 2006; Çirakman 2002; Harper 2011.
4   For an excellent study of early modern European perceptions of the Mughals see Sapra 2011.
5   For early modern perceptions of the Safavids see Mathee 2009.
6   Matar 2003: 9. For bin Qasim see also Wiegers 1992. Despite its ubiquity, the term 'Turk' was not even a very accurate label for an inhabitant of the Ottoman empire as it disguised the diversity of religious, ethnic and linguistic groups within it. The term was used by the Ottomans themselves to refer specifically to the Anatolian peasants (MacLean 2007: 6). There were, of course, knowledgeable exceptions to this undifferentiated picture of early modern Islam. See, for example, Sir Henry Blount's *Voyage into the Levant* where he noted the different forms of Islam practised by Tartars, Moors, Arabs, Persians and Turks (Blount 1636: 80).

concerns are much more modest. Although there is a remarkable range of possible data from throughout Europe which could allow us to examine the reception of Islam within, for example, the early modern Portuguese,[7] Swedish[8] or Hapsburg empires,[9] or, say, amongst the Dutch,[10] Venetians[11] or Maltese,[12] we shall investigate perceptions of Islam in England[13] and her colonies, and, even more specifically, the reception of Islam in the writing and experience of the early Quakers (or, more formally, the Religious Society of Friends).[14] Indeed, our focus is narrower still, and is concerned with scrutinizing the striking and paradoxical images of Islam that emerged, in part, as a consequence of early Quaker experience of so-called Barbary slavery in the last quarter of the seventeenth century.

At first sight this might appear an inconsequential subject of study. Despite their considerable notoriety in the seventeenth century,[15] not only in England and the British Isles, but also in mainland Europe and the American colonies, where they soon had a prominent literal, and,

---

7   Barletta 2010; Blackmore 2009; Garces 2011.

8   Ådahl 2006.

9   Fichtner 2008.

10 Steenbrink 2006.

11 Carboni 2007; Setton 1991.

12 See Ciappara 2004.

13 The Act of Union was not until 1707 and so what follows is not about Britain *per se*. Scottish experience of Barbary slavery was limited and similarly there are few Welsh present in our sources.

14 The label 'Quaker' was first given to the movement by a judge, Justice Bennett, when its most prominent figure, George Fox, was tried for blasphemy at Derby in 1650 (Fox 1694: 37). 'Friends' was the commonest self-designation (see John 15:14) though they also called themselves by other names including 'Children of Light', 'Saints', 'People of God' (see Moore 2000: 132). The term 'Quaker' was used before it was applied to Friends, most notably of a group of foreign women in Southwark in 1647 who were said to 'swell, shiver, and shake' under the inspiration of 'Mahomet's Holy Ghost' (Braithwaite 1955: 57). The report we have does not mean that these women were thought to be Muslims as Muhammad's inspiration was commonly believed in England to have been a result of epilepsy – an anti-Islamic calumny that originated in the eighth century – and was regarded as the paradigmatic example of religious fraud (see Edwards 1647: 180; Ross 1649: 398; see Dimmock 2013).
The language could well be intended to be pejorative rather than descriptive. The ecstatic inspiration of Friends, and specifically George Fox, and the inspiration of Muhammad, were often compared, in order to malign both (Leslie 1698: 15; Anon. 1712: 29).

15 Reay 1980; Miller 2005.

even greater, imaginative presence,[16] Quakers were always numerically insignificant, numbering by the end of the seventeenth century not more than 100,000 and probably considerably less[17] (to help contextualise this, England had a population of about five million in the late seventeenth century).[18]

The perceptions of Islam held by this one, small, heterodox Christian sect, might well seem a rather obscure subject to examine, particularly when compared, for example, with the construction of Islam in, say, the works of Luther, which is clearly of far greater historical consequence.[19] It is also the case that Quakers do not lend themselves easily to those who wish to use the past to assist in understanding the religious or political exigencies of the modern world – a significant motivation behind much contemporary scholarship concerned with the analysis of the relationship between Christians and Muslims.[20] Quakers in the seventeenth century were an eccentric and marginal religious group, untypical of most forms of Christianity in the period, in fact intentionally so. Friends presented themselves as a self-consciously 'peculiar people'[21] that strove to be unrepresentative of other Christians.

Indeed, given that early Quakerism is unfamiliar to most of those with an interest in the study of inter-religious relations, and its distinctive form of Christianity is central to understanding its encounter with Muslims and Islam, it is important to begin our analysis with a brief sketch of the origins and core characteristics of the Quaker movement in the seventeenth century.

---

16 See Ryan 2009: 27–62.
17 Reay puts the figure at 60,000 in England and Wales by the mid-1660s (Reay 1985: 11, 26–29) and Braithwaite at about 40,000 (1955: 512). John Gaskin, a contemporary critic of Quakers, put the number at about 30,000 in 1660 (1660: iv), Francis Bugg, another vociferous critic put the figure at 100,000 in 1699 (Bugg 1699: 1). See also Davies 2000: 156–67.
18 Grigg 1980: 84. It should be noted that by the 1660s Quakers were not only found in England but also Wales and, as Gaskin observed, 'in Ireland, Scotland, Barbadus [sic], and new England, Holland, and other places.' (1660: v).
19 Bobzin 1985; Brecht 2000; Ehmann 2008; Francisco 2007.
20 See, for example, Menocal 2002.
21 See, for example, Fox 1698: 488 (Ep. 383). The English expression is also found in Deuteronomy 14:2, Titus 2:14, 1 Peter 2:9 (King James Version). In context the phrase describes the distinctive people of God.

2. Early Quakerism

Early Quaker beliefs and practices have been categorized by scholars in a variety of ways, with some categorizations rather more helpful than others. Early Friends have, for example, been variously described as Puritans, millenarians, Boehmist mystics, a Holiness movement,[22] and proto-Pentecostals.[23] Any brief summary runs the risk of being homogenizing and essentialising, but it is relatively uncontroversial to say that Quakerism had its origins during the turmoil of the English Revolution[24] and contained, long after the Restoration in 1660, elements of the religious radicalism and social innovation that were characteristic of some groups within it[25] – as well as some of their most notable personnel.[26] The movement began in the English midlands in the 1640s but only became a visible, identifiable group in 1652 in the north of England, when a significant number of people were galvanized by the message proclaimed by such figures as Elizabeth Hooton, Richard Farnworth, William Dewsbury, James Nayler, but most famously George Fox.[27] A period of intensive activity followed which Rosemary Moore quite rightly calls an 'explosion',[28] as the movement rapidly expanded, first in England and Wales in 1653, then throughout the rest of the British Isles by 1654, before reaching mainland Europe,

---

22 Endy 1981; Hamm 1993; Ingle 1987; Spencer 2007: 39–58.

23 For parallels with Pentecostalism see Burgess and Maas 2002.

24 Though dated, Hill 1972, remains the best guide to the radical ideas of the English Revolution. The 'English Revolution' refers to the period of the Civil Wars and the Commonwealth, from 1640–1660, though the usefulness of this particular periodisation has been criticised (see Richardson 1998; Woolrych 2002).

25 See, for example, Thomas 1958: 44. However, much of the political radicalism was lost within the first decade (see Hill 1984: 129–69). For a useful discussion of the critical issues around the use of 'radicalism' to discuss early modern movements see Hessayon and Finnegan 2011.

26 Most famously perhaps, the former Leveller, John Lilburne, and former Digger, Gerrard Winstanley.

27 The classic, comprehensive treatment of this period remains Braithwaite 1955, though see also Moore 2000.

28 Moore 2000: 22–34.

the Americas, and the Caribbean, in the subsequent year.[29] Within a few years of the inception of the movement, Quakers were proclaiming their message from Newfoundland to Constantinople, from Surinam to Geneva.

There were variations, inconsistencies and developments in the way the core ideas of the new movement were articulated, particularly in the first decade,[30] and their opponents complained, with some justification, that key terms and metaphors employed by the Quakers were used in a multitude of often imprecise and conflicting ways.[31] This complaint remained a legitimate one despite the plethora of works Friends produced to answer their critics,[32] and even after the publication in 1676 of Robert Barclay's *Apology*, a systematic exposition of the new faith by a Quaker with considerable formal training in theology, something that many of the initial figures in the movement, such as Fox and Nayler, lacked.[33] In part the problem lay with early Quakerism itself, which was fundamentally experiential, and proclaimed a message predicated upon the conviction that everyone has the capacity to experience the direct, unmediated, transformative and ongoing presence of God through responding to the Seed[34] or Light of Christ within,[35] something that does not need

---

29 See Braithwaite 1955: 401–433. For a Quaker perspective on this period, see Fox's account in Cadbury 1972: 8–46; Fox 1694; Sewel 1722 and the local Quaker accounts collected in Penney 1907. See also Croese 1696.

30 For a useful analysis of this see Moore 2000: 75–87.

31 John Faldo, for example, a critic of early Quakers, complained about their 'unintelligible phrases' (1673: 61) and, in particular, the novel meanings they found in familiar biblical vocabulary. He felt it necessary to publish a key based upon the writings of prominent Quakers, although he still despaired of making sense of them. Faldo listed 34 meanings of 'the light within' in early Quakerism and still believed that he had not exhausted all of its possible uses in the writings of Friends (1673: 71).

32 See, for example, Baxter 1655; Higginson 1653; Gaskin 1660. For a sense of the extent of anti-Quaker writings, and early Quaker responses, see Smith 1873.

33 Barclay's *Apology* was initially published in Latin. The first English edition was published in 1678.

34 This metaphor is used a number of ways in early Quakerism. For a helpful analysis of the metaphorical range of the term 'seed' in Fox's *Journal* see Pickvance 1989: 116–118. Where the metaphor referred to an inward state, the idea was predominately Christological and its meaning derived from the promise in Genesis 3:15, that the seed of Eve would 'crush the serpent's head', reversing the experience of the fall. For a typical example of early Quaker use, see Fox 1694: 9 (cf. Romans 16:20).

35 Friends used a range of metaphors to relate this experience. For useful discussions of early Quaker understandings of the 'light' see Gwyn 1986: 65–91; Moore 2000:

any external rituals, clergy or creeds and which is, in fact, antithetical to all these things and all outward forms of religious faith.[36] Such experience, Quakers claimed, would assure, empower and guide those who were obedient to it, leading them to perfection, and gathering them into a new, distinctive, people of God.[37] This idea is encapsulated well in the response of the leading Quaker, Richard Hubberthorn, to Charles II when asked to explain the 'principle' of Quakerism in 1660:

> Our Principle is this, That Jesus Christ is the true Light which enlightneth everyone that cometh into the world;[38] that all men through him might believe; and that they are to obey and follow this light, as they have received it, whereby they may be led unto God and unto Righteousness, and the knowledge of the truth, that they may be saved.[39]

Their initial gospel was at its heart an apocalyptic one:[40] they claimed that they were living at a particular moment when God's Spirit was now poured out on all people, both men and women, as had been prophesied in the book of Joel.[41] As the anonymous author of the early anti-Quaker tract *Querers and Quakers* of 1653 complained, according to the Quakers 'men, women, boys and girls, may all turn into prophets'.[42] God, for them, now taught everyone directly. They were convinced that all people

---

81–87. Egg-Olofsson 1954 is also helpful although specifically focused upon Robert Barclay's later theological systematization of the concept.

36 Though they could, on occasion, express themselves in language reminiscent of the traditional creeds of Christianity. Fox, for example, could write to the governor of Barbados with words that echoed the Apostles' and Nicene creeds, albeit within an overtly Quaker letter. See Fox 1672: 65–79; 1694: 358–361.

37 Indeed, an early and influential corporate statement by Quakers, the *Epistle of the Elders of Balby* (1656) addresses the problem of inspiration 'out of the Light' and how the fledgling communities should deal with people whose behaviour or prophecy was in conflict with the collective witness of Friends (Barclay 1841: 277–282).

38 A quotation from John 1:9 and one beloved by early Friends as evidence that all people contained this capacity.

39 Hubberthorn 1660: 3.

40 The best exposition of this apocalyptic interpretation of Quaker thought is Gwyn 1986. See also the important recent work of Guiton 2012.

41 Acts 2:17; Joel 2:28. See, for example, Barclay 1673: 88; Burrough 1657: 11; Fell 1655: 13; 1666: 13; Fox 1653: 44; 1656b: 1; 1661a: 5.

42 Anon. 1653. Moore (2000) and Carroll (1978, 2008) provide useful discussions of early Quaker prophetic motivation and compulsion.

should now worship God directly 'in spirit and in truth',[43] and women and men should gather to wait upon God and experience direct inspiration from the Spirit; all other kinds of worship were now redundant. Again, a quotation from one of their early leaders, William Dewsbury, illustrates this well:

> To you the mighty Day of the Lord is coming and in His power is appearing amongst you, in raising desires in some of you towards His name, which desires cannot be satisfied with any outward observations and traditions of your fathers...the glad tidings of the gospel of eternal salvation is heard within, in this day of the Lord's mercy, wherin he is teaching His people Himself.[44]

Practically speaking, Quaker worship took place wherever Quakers were able to gather though it was particularly associated with a 'Meeting' of Friends, a group of Quakers usually related to a specific location, and who, from early in the history of the movement, gathered for mutual admonition and support as well as worship in the more conventional sense (early Friends were keen that distinctions were not drawn between such activities). Initially domestic space seems to have been the common place for Quakers to gather but they soon acquired 'Meeting Houses', which were either adapted commercial or domestic properties or, from the 1670s, were purpose-built. Early Quakers viewed such buildings as entirely utilitarian and they reflected the movement's aniconic convictions and culture.[45]

Friends rejected 'apostate Christendom' in all its forms[46] but particularly its professional representatives. Not only did they refuse to pay the tithe, or church tax, but in their early years they regularly disrupted church services and harangued ministers and priests whom they called 'hireling shepherds',[47] and, at times, much worse;[48] judging them venal

---

43 In fulfilment of Jesus' words to the Samaritan woman in John 4:23. See, for example, Fox 1654. Such belief in direct, charismatic inspiration led to a manner of worship that was disturbing to their contemporaries. See, for example, Higginson 1653: 12.

44 Dewsbury 1689: 156 (the original text was written in 1656).

45 See Butler 1999: 888–889.

46 For a typical example of this see Burrough 1657.

47 John 10:12. See, for example, Fox 1664: 62.

48 Mary Fisher, for example, was not unusual in shouting at the minister in Selby in

peddlers of learning without true knowledge.[49] Although the Bible was central to early Quaker religious life and self-understanding,[50] their belief in immediate revelation and the sufficiency of the indwelling Light meant that they emphasised the superiority and presence of the living Word, Christ,[51] over the 'words of God'[52] that were found in scripture. Indeed, they claimed that they experienced the Spirit that 'gave forth the scriptures' and without this the Bible could not be read correctly.[53] Although they were adamant that they did not reject scripture, it is perhaps unsurprising that they were regularly accused of doing so.[54]

Quakers also developed, from the outset, a range of distinctive cultural practices, which are usefully characterised by Richard Bauman as a 'rhetoric of impoliteness',[55] that became both indicative and symbolic of the religious convictions of the movement and separated them from their contemporaries (not least by provoking sharp reactions from non-Quakers). Chief amongst these were their refusal to swear oaths, to close their businesses on the sabbath or during religious festivals (including Christmas), to use greetings or deferential titles of address,[56] to remove their hats (notably to their social superiors), and their insistence on us-

---

1652, 'Come downe, come downe, thou painted beast, come downe. Thou art but a hireling, and deluder of the people with thy lyes' (see Villani 2004).

49 A number of early Friends were themselves ex-ministers such as the erudite Samuel Fisher.

50 It was famously said by one of the chroniclers of the early Quakers, the Reformed minister Gerardus Croese, that 'though the Bible were lost, it might be found in the mouth of George Fox', such was the reputation Fox had for scriptural allusion and quotation, something common to Friends in the seventeenth century (Croese 1696: 14). Barbour claims that approximately 70 percent of all early Quaker writing took the form of quotations, allusions or paraphrases of biblical verses (1964: 157).

51 Texts such as Hebrews 4:12 and John 1:1 and 9 were important in their defence of this position.

52 Fox 1694: 102.

53 See Fox 1694: 22–23.

54 See Underwood 1997: 20–33. To be fair to the opponents of Quakerism, some Quakers actively sought to undermine the authority of the text of the Bible to demonstrate the superiority of the indwelling Light, as we can see most clearly in Samuel Fisher's substantial work of radical biblical criticism, *Rusticus ad Academicos* (1660), a work by an author closely associated with Baruch Spinoza. See Champion 1999; Frampton 2007: 217–222; Hill 1972: 259–68; Popkin 1985.

55 Bauman 1983: 43.

56 See, for example, Fox 1657.

ing 'Thee' and 'Thou' as the second person singular rather than 'You' (in part because it implied a distinction in social class),[57] though there were other forms of behaviour, including plain style in dress and speech, that also became a significant part of Quaker identity. Although this was not uniform at the outset, by the late 1650s they would also become known for their pacifism.[58] They justified these behaviours in a range of ways but they were all taken as evidence of their identity as God's distinctive and separate people.[59]

In time, particularly after the scandal of the trial of James Nayler before Parliament for blasphemy in 1656[60] and the promulgation of clear, centralised structures within the movement from 1666 that subordinated the inspired individual to the corporate authority of the church,[61] Quakerism's oppositional apocalypticism was moderated.[62] Despite the

---

57 See, for example, Fox 1660b.

58 Although it has now become customary to assume that the development of pacifism as a core component of Quaker identity and practice was something that happened following the Restoration (see Reay 1985: 106-107, 121), as a stratagem for survival in the face of political 'defeat' (Hill 1984: 129–169; Bauman 1983: 118–119) this does not do justice to the evidence, as Greaves 1992 has shown; and given the rigours of Quaker pacifism and its consequences for individual Quakers, it would hardly be the easiest or most effective means of demonstrating Quaker loyalty to the new status quo. Despite some exceptions, such as those Quakers who became involved in Monmouth's rebellion of 1685 (Hill 1984: 162) and King Philip's War against Native Americans in New England of 1675–78 (Weddle 2001), Quaker pacifism became virtually universal following the Restoration – and Fox could boast in 1667 that 'swordsmen' could no longer be found amongst them (Fox 1667b: 9). For useful discussions of this subject see Guiton 2012: 334—368; Jones 1984; Weddle 2001.

59 Zephaniah 3:9–13. The best exploration of this Quaker culture is Bauman 1983, but see also Hinds 2011. For an influential summary and defence of such behaviour see Penn 1669.

60 See Bittle 1986; Damrosch 1996; Deacon 1656.

61 Seen, for example, in the *Epistle of the Brethren* (1666) found in Barclay 1841: 318–324. Braithwaite 1979: 247–268.

62 This is the position argued by Braithwaite 1955; Ingle 1994; Moore 2000; Reay 1985. Some of the more extreme forms of behaviour, such as 'going naked as a sign', ceased altogether (see Carroll 1978; Simpson 1660); Friends were influenced by biblical precedents for such actions, such as the behaviour of the prophet Isaiah (see Isaiah 20:3–4). Some of other charismatic practices continued though on a diminished scale, such as the claim that miracles, especially miracles of healing, accompanied and confirmed Quaker activity. Whilst Fox's *Journal*, when first published in 1694, did include a number of healings, they are very limited in comparison to his 'Book of Miracles', a collection of 176 miracles but which the Society decided not to publish, and which has only survived as an index. See Fox 2000.

constant if sporadic persecution, both *de jure* and *de facto*, that continued until the Act of Toleration of 1689, when it was significantly alleviated,[63] with time Quakers became less actively confrontational and more broadly accepted by their peers.[64] Nonetheless, it is important to realise, for the purposes of this essay, that these changes should not be exaggerated: although Quakerism underwent a number of developments during the seventeenth century, the core cluster of distinctive religious convictions and identifiable practices we have just detailed remained more or less consistent throughout the period and throughout the movement. This owed itself, in part, to the dominance of George Fox who was not only one of the key figures in the birth of the movement, but held considerable charismatic authority within it until his death in 1691. The vigorous print culture Friends fostered also helped ensure the continuity of ideas and practices within early Quakerism,[65] and the development of vibrant local, national and international Quaker networks, consolidated by ties of trade and kinship (Quakerism soon became a strictly endogamous sect), and regular travel and communication between Meetings, created a Quaker culture that varied little from place to place, from Barbados to Aberdeen, or Pennsylvania to Colchester, until the late eighteenth century.[66] Some Quaker beliefs and practices, such as the notion that women as well as men could preach, were not unique to them,[67] but they were unusual in sustaining such ways of thinking and behaving, and making them central to their faith. As we see from the following quote by Richard Baxter, a famous Puritan divine, writing in the 1690s, those outside the movement believed that Quakerism during the period upon which we shall focus remained essentially unchanged from that which had emerged in the 1640s.

---

63 See Ayoub 2005; Coffey 2000: 151–155, 168–179; Davies 2000; Horle 1988. For a study of post-1689 persecution see Allen 2003.
64 See Davies 2000: 11, 221.
65 Corns and Loewenstein 1996; Peters 2005.
66 See Tolles 1963b: ix; Gragg 2009.
67 Davies 1986; Mack 1994.

They make the light which every man have within him to be his sufficient rule, and consequently the Scripture and ministry are set light by . . . they pretend their dependence on the Spirit's conduct against set times of prayer and against sacrament, and against their due esteem of Scripture and ministry; they will not have the Scripture called the word of God; their principal zeal lieth in railing at the ministers as hirelings, deceivers, false prophets, etc., and in refusing to swear before a magistrate, or put off their hat to any, or say 'You' instead of 'Thou' or 'Thee', which are their words to all.[68]

Nevertheless, however unusual, unrepresentative and marginal, early Quakers might be, the subject of this essay can be justified in a number of ways. Geoffrey Cantor's study of the parallel responses of British Quakers and British Jews to modernity and science,[69] which demonstrates that both actively and rapidly took up and championed Darwinian ideas,[70] contrary to many assumptions about the inexorable conflict between religion and science, is illustrative of the wider value of studies of minority religious dissent and the need for them to break free of the claustrophobic world of denominational scholarship. What follows could also be seen as an exercise in microhistory, of a necessary reduction in the scale of observation in order to engage in intensive documentary scrutiny which allows us to 'ask large questions in small places' as Charles Joyner put it.[71] Such work often runs the risk of being labelled 'trivia' but, as Chartier rightly says, 'it is on the reduced scale, and probably only on this scale, that we can understand without deterministic reduction, the relationship between systems of belief, of values, of representations on one side and social affiliations on the other'.[72]

Indeed, not only, as we shall see, do the early Quaker records provide us with surprising and disruptive narratives which regularly, if not com-

---

68 Baxter 1696: 73–74, 77. See also Bugg (1703: 43–44). Bugg acknowledged that Friends were now more respected and less confrontational, but he was adamant that their beliefs remained as heretical as they ever had been.
69 Cantor 2005.
70 Cantor 2005: 357.
71 See Joyner 1999: 1.
72 Chartier quoted in Brooks et al. 2008: 5.

prehensively, question our expectations of the nature of early modern interpretations of Islam, providing much that is anomalous and paradoxical, but they also encourage us to reflect on more general questions about the alleged immutability and inevitability of representations of Islam in the West,[73] and the place of apocalyptic in this. The latter is usually seen as something that at best radically constrains inter-religious encounters, rendering them of fleeting consequence, functioning to negate the worth of non-Christians included within apocalyptic scenarios, reducing them to temporary, expendable and lumpen figures in a triumphant, Christian drama.[74] In the Quaker narratives, apocalyptic appears to engender and valorise the encounter, reflected in the surprising images and practices generated, as much because of what it does to the Christian subject as to how it transforms the Muslim object.

The words of reproach of the prophet Zechariah, so popular amongst early Friends as an expression of the apocalyptic revaluing of the everyday as the site for the immediate encounter with God, and a warrant for their belief that the transforming presence of God lay in all people, may provide us with a justification of our focus on this apparently obscure subject: 'For who hath despised the day of small things?'[75]

---

73 Vitkus claims, for example, an 'unbroken tradition' of polemical representations of Islam from the early modern to the modern West' (1999: 226).
74 Matar 1998a: 153–183; Setton 1992. For the Muslim analogue of such thinking, see Krstić 2011: 75–97.
75 Zechariah 4:10. See, for example, Crook 1662: 20; Farnworth 1653: 30; Fell 1668: 33; Penington 1661: 35.

3. Barbary Slavery

However, before we progress any further, it is important to say something of Barbary slavery, the context within which the records we will examine were generated. Barbary slavery is not necessarily widely known today,[76] despite its cultural prominence in early modern Europe and the numbers involved: a million to a million and quarter Europeans, from the early sixteenth to the eighteenth century, found themselves sold in the slave markets of North Africa.[77]

Although the involvement of Britons in the Atlantic slave trade, which entailed the enslavement of far greater numbers of Africans and their transportation to the Americas and the Caribbean, is familiar to most,[78] outside of a few corners of south west England, particularly Cornwall, and some historians of the early modern period, Barbary slavery is largely forgotten in the anglophone world.[79] The victims of Barbary slavers were primarily taken by privateers from the independent kingdom of Morocco and the Ottoman regencies of Algeria, Tunisia and Libya (Tripolitania), a region that roughly equates with what is known today as the Maghreb, but which was referred to by the early modern English as 'Barbary', a word that reveals something of the disdain felt towards its inhabitants

---

76 For recent studies that discuss Barbary slavery see Davis 2001, 2003, 2009; Friedman 1983; Jamieson 2012; MacLean and Matar 2011: 124–155; Matar 2005; Tinniswood 2010; Vitkus 2001; Weiss 2011.

77 Although, as Davis is keen to point out, this is a rough approximation and we lack the kind of detailed records that we have for the transatlantic trade in Africans, a subject that has also benefited from half a century of scrutiny (2009: 60). Davis' estimate has been contested by Matar (2005: 207). For a description of the slave markets see D'Aranda 1666:7–9.

78 The total number of Africans shipped across the Atlantic is difficult to determine but probably amounted to about twelve million. See Curtin 1969; Lovejoy 1989.

79 It is somewhat better known in the United States of America because of its significance in the formative years of that nation. Following independence from Britain, American shipping suddenly became vulnerable to corsair activity as it ceased to be protected by treaties agreed between the British Empire and the North African powers. This led to the two Barbary wars, the first against Tripoli (1801–1805), and the second, against Algiers (1815). See Lambert 2005.

(though its etymology is somewhat problematic and had its root in classical and Arabic terminology).[80] The phenomenon, or rather the cultural representation of the phenomenon, had a significant, even determinative, effect upon European perceptions of Islam in the early modern period, including that of the English, shaping the way 'generations of English men and women thought about Muslims and the Islamic world'.[81]

Barbary slavery was a very international experience, as is evident in the following remark by Pierre Dan who visited the Barbary Coast in 1634:

> As to the slaves of both sexes that are in Barbary today, there are a quantity of them from all the Christian nations, such as France, Italy, Spain, England, Germany, Flanders, Holland, Greece, Hungary, Poland, Slovenia, Russia and so forth.[82]

In terms of absolute scale, the Italian, Spanish or French slaves were the most numerous in the Barbary states, although in terms of relative scale, the Icelanders probably lost the largest percentage of their population, with hundreds enslaved in a cataclysmic raid of 1627,[83] an event that has

---

80 The term probably derives from the Latin *barbaria* and the Greek *barbaros* which were used to refer to those who were uncivilised, although in classical writings it was never employed to designate either the region of the Maghreb or its inhabitants. It seems likely that the classical term was adopted by Arab speakers who referred to non-Arabic speaking Muslim inhabitants of Africa as *al-barbar* although with a rather broader range of connotations. We can see this, for example, in the writings of the fourteenth-century travel writer Ibn Battutah, who used the term to refer to African Muslims whom he judged to be at some cultural distance from Arab Muslim culture of which he was a member – although he was, himself, from the Maghreb (see Hall 2005: 340). The term was not, however, used for the region of north west Africa in North African Arabic or Turkish languages (Matar 2005: 3). The first use of the word 'Barbary' in English to refer to the North African coast is found in Shakespeare's *Merchant of Venice* III. ii. 267 (1600), although variations of the term (*Barbaria, Barbarie*) had been used in continental Europe for some time before this.

81 MacLean and Matar 2011: 124.

82 Dan1646: 320. Dan was a Redemptionist priest, a member of the The Order of the Most Holy Trinity, the Trinitarians, established in 1198. The other Redemptionist order was that of Our Lady of Mercy, the Mercedarians, established around 1218. Both orders were initially founded to respond to the needs of those Christians captured during the Crusades but in the early modern period they focused their attentions on the victims of Barbary slavery.

83 See Eigilssen 1641 (Egilsson 2008). D'Aranda noted the presence of the Icelanders in Algiers and their pitiful state (1666: 248).

left an enduring mark on Icelandic cultural memory.[84] Approximately five to ten percent of the Barbary slaves appear to have been from the British Isles, virtually all from England[85] or its nascent colonies in the West Indies and North America, although the actual figures fluctuated, increasing as English presence in the Atlantic and Mediterranean increased, and corsairs ventured further afield. Initially restricted by the range of galleys, the adoption of full-rigged tall ships from the early 1600s[86] allowed Barbary privateers to seize vessels and people in the Atlantic and North Sea, and even the Irish Sea and English Channel, taking sailors, merchants, travellers, colonists and fishermen from around the British Isles and throughout the English Atlantic possessions, from Barbados to Newfoundland to Ireland.

However, we should not forget that the North Africans themselves were also often the victims of slavers; 'as Christians feared the Barbary corsairs, Muslims feared the European corsairs.'[87] Although, unlike the European captives, the fate of these slaves has largely gone unnoticed as they did not produce captivity narratives of the kind that made such an impression throughout Europe[88] (there was no print culture amongst Ottoman Muslims until the late 18th century)[89] and much of our data about them is fragmentary.[90] Indeed Matar has made the important criticism

---

84 Lewis 1993; Helgasson 1995, 1997.

85 See Davies 2009: 37.

86 See Jamieson 2012: 85.

87 Matar 2003: xxviii.

88 However, we do have some accounts of Muslims who found themselves victims of the Atlantic slave trade. See Al-Ahari 2006; Bluet 1734. For a useful recent study of Muslim slaves in an early modern European city see Nadalo's study of Livorno (2011).

89 Gdoura 1985. There was no printing in Ottoman Turkish or Arabic until 1727 and even then no sustained activity until the end of that century as this first attempt to establish a press by Ibrahim Müteferrika (a Hungarian Unitarian convert and former slave) was shortlived, ending in 1742 (Gencer 2008). However, the first Hebrew press was established in 1494 and first Armenian press in 1597. This prohibition on printing was well known in early modern England, and Henry Oldenburg, the first secretary of the Royal Society, saw it as a sign of Ottoman 'despotism' and a result of the fear that the ideas that it would help disseminate would lead to the kind of divisions that beset Christendom (Briggs and Burke 2010: 14).

90 There are exceptions to this. There are, for example, sufficient records to reconstruct something of the efforts of free Muslims (Mudejars) of Christian Valencia to redeem co-religionists from enslavement in Spain in the fifteenth century, though

of Colley who argued that the captivity of male and female Britons and others was the price paid for the imperial project of European nations, remarking:

> There is no denying the extensive North African piracy and privateering against Britons and other Europeans in the early modern period. But finding the price of the European empires – specifically the British, and, by the same token, the Spanish, Portuguese and French – chiefly in the suffering of Christian captives seized by the "natives" is to invoke Eurocentrism that produces an inaccurate and lopsided view of historical development – and one that, since Braudel's magisterial survey of the Mediterranean – is not defensible.[91]

He quite rightly notes that we must take into account the slave markets in, for example, Genoa, Cadiz, Malta, Livorno, Venice, Naples, Barcelona, Marseilles and Valencia, which specialised in the sale of Muslims.[92] One needs only see the statue of Duke Ferdinando I in Livorno, originally erected in 1617 but now known as *Il monumento dei Quattro mori* because of the addition, a few years later, of four chained, bronze Moors, to be reminded of this.[93] We should see Barbary slavery as a reciprocal phenomenon,[94] and part of a more general Mediterranean slavery, deeply entwined with the ambitions and actions of all parties, in which no particular nation or religion was the victim. So, for example, in 1624 the ruler of Algiers explained to James I that:

---

this should also be understood in the context of a related but rather different context of struggles between and amongst Christians and Muslims in the Iberian peninsula (see Meyerson 1996; van Koningsveld 1995). Miller makes the interesting case that 'Mudejars community action reconfigured jihad as slave liberation and captive redemption' (Miller 2008: 175).

91 Matar 2005: 111–112.

92 Nor, indeed, should we forget the existence of Portuguese and Spanish enclaves, or *presidios*, in North Africa, which were key to the acquisition and trade in North African slaves, notably Ceuta, Melilla, Peñón de Vélez de la Gomera, Oran, Larache, La Mamora and Mazagan (see Driessen 1992). Indeed, from 1662 to 1684 the English colony of Tangiers had a similar function in the slave economy, before its inordinate cost led to its being abandoned. For example, in 1682, 250 Algerian slaves were shipped there (Matar 2005: 127). See also Chappell 1935; Aylmer 1999.

93 The statue made an impression on contemporaries. See, for example, Egilsson (2008: 56).

94 Weiss 2011: 170. See also Braudel 1973: 868.

Your majesties subjects did take some Moores, and Turkes; and now our Captaines did take certain Englishmen, and sold them; which if your Majestie shall be pleased to send us the Moores and Turkes, Wee shall suddainly and out of hand putt the Christians att Liberty.[95]

In fact both Christian and Muslim rulers supported Barbary privateers and, from time to time, cooperated in suppressing them, depending upon the vagaries of political alliances which were not circumscribed by religion[96] and often underwent rapid change. Barbary corsairs, of whatever origin, were often as much a menace to 'Muslim' shipping as 'Christian'. Indeed, as William Okeley, an English victim of the corsairs, declared:

it is not evident that they would engage against Christian more than all the rest of Mankind, for all the World are their enemies, who are rich enough to invite them and too weak to resist them.[97]

Indeed, given that such slavery was so clearly and firmly embedded in the economy of the Mediterranean, it is unwise of Davis' to argue that we should refer to it as 'Faith' slavery,[98] and claim that it was a manifestation of an alleged incessant and essential conflict between 'Christianity' and 'Islam'.[99] One needs only examine the fate of Protestant slaves in Catholic galleys, such as the Englishman William Davies who wrote an account of the eight and half years he spent as such a slave in Livorno,[100] or, say, the seizing of an English (Protestant) ship carrying Muslim pilgrims on their way to hajj in 1651[101] by Maltese (Catholic) privateers to see that

---

95 Matar 2001: 10.
96 Matar 1999: 20–21. See Thompson 1994.
97 Okeley 1675: 13.
98 Davis 2009.
99 Davis somewhat simplistically argues that a 'holy war, or jihad, that was waged intermittently between the two worlds is well known – it began even before the Crusades of the 11th century and has lasted up to the present' (Davis 2009: vii). For a similar characterisation see Jamieson who describes Barbary corsairs as motivated by the notion that they were engaged in an 'eternal war' between Christians and the lands of Islam (2012: 11). For a contrary view see Clarence-Smith 2006: 28–30.
100 Davies 1617.
101 This incident ultimately resulted in the conversion of the Moroccan prince Baldassarre Loyola de Mandes, who would become an influential Jesuit. See Blunt 1951:

things are rather more complex. For those slavers who did have a religious motivation, such as those from a Morisco background,[102] this was essentially dependent upon a feeling of injustice and desire for revenge against those who had wronged them, or the need to demonstrate loyalty to their newly found or rediscovered faith, rather than any intrinsic or essential hostility towards non-Muslims.

159–166; Castries 1928; and the recent, definitive study of Colombo 2011. For a similar incident in 1688 see Matar 2005: 130.

102 Moriscos were expelled from Spain between 1609 and 1614 and the next three decades saw a significant rise in the number of corsair raids on the Spanish mainland (Friedman 1983: 12–13). In the history of al-Maqiri we are told that the Moriscos' 'sea-borne jihad is now famous' (Matar 2001: 12). Although Jónsson (2007) has noted that of the 300,000 or so expelled, only a very small number took part in corsairing of any kind.

4. Representations of Islam
in Early Modern Europe

Although we shall be focusing upon early modern English representations of Islam, it is important to contextualise our discussion by briefly
noting the prevailing assumptions about Islam in Europe at the time of
which these were a constituent part. It would be fair to say that the picture presented in Norman Daniel's influential *Islam and the West* remains
dominant, despite over half a century having passed since it was first
published; its basic thesis could be said to be restated in, for example,
Minou Reeves' *Muhammad in Europe: A Thousand Years of Western Myth-
Making*, published in 2003.[103] Daniel argues that an essentially hostile
image of Islam and Muslims was forged during the Crusades and endured,
with little change, until relatively recently.[104] This consisted of a canon of
views about what constituted Islam, derived from a recurring, immutable
cluster of pejorative judgements and traditions about the life and morality of its prophet, the nature of its revealed text, and the character and
worship of its adherents. European 'knowledge' of Islam was largely dependent upon legendary fabrications and was impervious to information
about the reality of Muslim faith and practice. Although Daniel does not
expend much time examining the early modern period, he does remark
on the continued prevalence of such ideas in sources from this epoch.
For example, he notes that Humphrey Prideaux's influential *The True
Nature of the Imposture Display'd* (1697) would leave 'the reader familiar
with the Middle Ages agape' because it was not only heavily dependent
upon the work of Riccoldo da Monte di Croce's polemical *Contra Legem
Sarracenorum*,[105] published in the early fourteenth century but 'outdoes
almost any mediaeval writer in its virulence'.[106]

The work of Edward Said, despite adding considerable analytical so-
phistication, essentially reiterates the picture presented by Daniel and

---

103 Reeves 2003.
104 Daniel 1993: 306.
105 For Riccoldo da Monte di Croce see George-Tvrtkovic 2007, 2013.
106 Daniel 1992: 309.

has helped shape much of contemporary scholarship.[107] Although his influential *Orientalism* goes beyond the question of how Islam was represented by Europeans, to examine, as the subtitle of the French edition concisely expresses it, *L'Orient créé par l'Occident,* nonetheless it repeats similar historiographical characterisations which can also be found in his later works, notably *Covering Islam.*[108] For Said, 'Orientalism' can mean a number of things. It can refer to an academic activity,[109] or a style of thought[110] but most importantly, for his analysis, it can describe a manner of dealing with the East:

> Dealing with it by making statements about it, authorizing views of it, describing it, by teaching it, settling it, ruling over it: in short Orientalism as a Western style for dominating, restructuring, and having authority over the Orient.[111]

It is an immutable ideology which is reflected in a very specific discursive construction of Islam:

> The European encounter with the Orient, and specifically with Islam ... turned Islam into the very epitome of an outsider against which the whole of European civilization from the Middle Ages on was founded.[112]

What exactly is the character of the 'Orient' created by the 'Occident'? For Said, the way that the Orient is described is 'always symmetrical to, and yet diametrically inferior to, a European equivalent.'[113] For exam-

---

107 See, for example, Said 2003: 60.

108 Said 1981; reissued with a fresh introduction 1997.

109 'Anyone who teaches, writes about, or researches the Orient – and this applies whether the person is an anthropologist, sociologist, historian or philologist – either in its specific or its general aspects, is an Orientalist, and what he or she does is Orientalism' (Said 2003: 2).

110 'Orientalism is a style of thought based upon an ontological and epistemological distinction made between "the Orient" and (most of the time) "the Occident"' (Said 2003: 2). 'This Orientalism can accommodate Aeschylus, say, and Victor Hugo, Dante and Karl Marx' (Said 2003: 3).

111 Said 2003: 3.

112 Said 1978: 70.

113 Said 1978: 72.

ple, Prideaux's biography of Muhammad[114] epitomises just such a way of thinking; Prideaux, could only make sense of Islam by seeing it as fraudulent, its founder an opposite to the key figure in Occidental culture – Jesus.[115] Although Said was mostly concerned with the post-Napoleonic world, and not the early modern, his perspective has helped reinforce a rather crude notion that the relationship between 'Europe' and the 'Muslim world' in this period was essentially thought of (from the European point of view) as one of 'a binary opposition between a civilized Christian "'West" and the encroaching barbarity of an infidel "East"'.[116] It is hard to underestimate the impact of Said's thought, and the book *Orientalism* continues to be a 'site of controversy, adulation and criticism'.[117] It is difficult now to imagine a world in which Said's ideas do not dominate or shape the fundamental presuppositions of many approaching the subject; for all its undoubted strengths, it has, as MacLean says, cast a long, long shadow.[118]

Before we proceed any further, I do not wish to be accused of misrepresenting the picture of Islam that Daniel and Said argue was dominant in European culture. Daniel was aware of exceptions to the prevailing images that he presented, noting, for example, in the early modern period, the work of Henry Stubbe,[119] an English deist who wrote a defence of the life of Muhammad and to which we will turn in a moment.[120] Even Said could famously champion proponents of 'antithetical knowledge'[121] of Islam, produced by those writing against the prevailing orthodoxy, from the margins, although he does not identify such 'knowledge' in the premodern world, restricting it to the productions of contemporary com-

---

114 Prideaux 1697.
115 Said 2003: 72.
116 Birchwood and Dimmock 2005: 1.
117 Ashcroft and Ahluwalia 2001: 49. The literature generated in response to Said's work is extensive. However, for trenchant criticisms of the theoretical framework of Said see, for example, Porter (1993); Ahmad (1992),
118 As MacLean rightly says, 'Perhaps the most regrettable effect of Said's important study has been that many scholars coming of age in the long shadow of Orientalism have felt free to dismiss the important historical studies produced by skilled and knowledgeable Orientalists' (2007: 10).
119 Daniel 1993: 309. For Stubbe see Birchwood 2007; Holt 1972; Jacob 1983.
120 Stubbe 1911. Stubbe's manuscript was originally written c.1673–1676.
121 Said 1997: 157.

mentators. And, of course, there have been exceptions and qualifications of the pictures represented by both Daniel and Said. Richard Southern[122] could, for example, point to exceptional 'moments of vision' evident in the lives of John Bacon, John of Segovia and Nicholas of Cusa which disturb the prevailing picture. In more recent years, there has been an interest in the narratives of Christian and Muslim (and Jewish) interaction in Al-Andalus,[123] and the Iberian Mozarabs,[124] stories which may disrupt the generalisations derived from Daniel and Said, and raise questions about what exactly constitutes the 'West'.

It is also worth noting that although much attention has been paid to the alleged role of the triumphalist, proto-colonialist 'gaze' of Christians, triumphalism was not a monopoly of Christian writers; it was something shared by Muslim authors too: 'all Muslim writers about Christendom were convinced that they possessed absolute religious truth and therefore were not dissimilar from each other in their sense of superiority to the Christians'.[125] Although, as Al-Azmeh has argued in his detailed analysis of Arabic ethnography from the medieval and early modern period, beyond some blanket assumptions about 'others' not being fellow believers and/or idolaters, expressly religious ways of viewing non-Muslims had little evaluative impact; representations were in fact 'governed by a natural-scientific ecological determinism mediated through the notions of humoral medicine'.[126]

---

122 Southern 1962.
123 Jayyusi 1994; Menocal 2002. Menocal, Scheindlin and Sells 2000.
124 Hitchcock 2008.
125 Matar 2009: 5.
126 Al-Azmeh 1992: 6. See also Al-Azmeh 1991.

5. Early Modern English Representations

In many ways, English representations of Islam in the early modern period appear to be typical of prevailing European discursive traditions.[127] Her colonists in the Americas and West Indies, closely embedded within an anglophone Atlantic culture and networks of governance, trade, religion and kinship, did not depart from these.[128] Indeed, Kidd's analysis of early modern American knowledge of Islam shows the same basic patterns that were present in early modern England, the continued republication of traditional, prejudicial tropes, and the avid consumption of a plethora of texts that contained them.[129] We should hesitate to describe the colonists or those in England as conversant with Islam but 'they certainly conversed about Islam regularly.'[130]

Although a number of texts could be used to illustrate early modern English receptions of Islam, three are particularly useful for our purposes, as they help map something of the prevailing characteristics of its image.

The first is Josua Poole's *The English Parnassus* (1657). This school textbook contains, amongst other things, a list of synonyms and epithets culled from 'the best authors' and is very revealing of assumptions about the 'Turke' in English culture. They were, needless to say, almost entirely pejorative. Under the entry for 'Turke' we find the words, 'unbelieving, misbelieving, thrifty, abstemious, cruel, unpitying, mercilesse, unrelenting, inexorable, warlick, circumcized, superstitious, bloody, wine-forbearing, turban'd, avaritious, covetous, erring'.[131]

---

127 Useful summaries can be found in Pailin 1984: 81–104, 198–222; MacLean and Matar 2011.

128 Indeed, as Fisher has demonstrated, the fundamental cultural patterns of the early colonists reflected the different regional, religious and social identities of waves of English settlers, taking the form of four distinct and distinguishable folkways (Fisher 1989).

129 Kidd 2003. See also Sha'ban 1991, 2005.

130 Kidd 2003: 766.

131 MacLean 2007: 7.

The second text is Humphrey Prideaux's *The True Nature of Imposture Displayed in the Life of Mahomet* (1697), to which we have already referred. This book, written by the Dean of Norwich Cathedral, is essentially a restatement of anti-Muslim traditions that date back to the Crusades and before – and includes customary accusations that Muhammad was a violent and corrupt charlatan, and his religion a diabolical parody of Christianity. For Prideaux, Muhammad's 'two prominent passions were *Ambition* and *Lust*. The course which he took to gain *Empire*, abundantly shows the former, and the multitude of women which he had to do with, proves the later.'[132] *The Nature of the Imposture* was remarkably popular and went through eight editions in England by 1723, and was widely published elsewhere, particularly in the North American colonies.[133]

The epithet 'impostor' was not one coined by Prideaux but had been used widely before in English writings, for example in Bedwell (1615) and Addison (1679). However, with Prideaux's book it became 'almost ubiquitous'.[134] The epithet reflects the fundamental problem that faced Christian interpretations of Islam. Unlike Judaism, which could be explained within a triumphalist Christian historical narrative, as something moribund and superseded, its persistence accounted for by reference to texts in which Jews were explicitly named and their fate detailed (for example, Romans 11:25), Islam had no obvious place in Christian scripture,[135] and was harder to comprehend. The finality of Christ meant that there was little theological warrant for making sense of the appearance and obvious success of its prophet other than to view him as a parody of Christ, sent to scourge a wayward Church.[136]

Prideaux's work is also important because, as its full title demonstrates, the book was 'offered to the consideration of the Deists of the present age.' It was not a work of history but, as Holt notes, clearly 'a tract for the times'.[137] As well as attacking Muhammad and his religion, Prideaux uses

---

132 Prideaux 1697: 137.
133 Kidd 2003: 766.
134 Kidd 2003: 766.
135 Despite its own claims, of which some in the early modern period were aware. See, for example, Stubbe 1911: 164.
136 Prideaux 1697: 13.
137 Holt 1998: 116–117.

the story of Muhammad to warn his readers about the consequences of allowing Socinians, Quakers and Deists to thrive in England; surely God will do to true Christianity what he did to the Eastern Churches, raise up another Muhammad to punish the church.[138] Prideaux also noted that Muhammad's assumption of the role of 'Impostor' occurred at the same time as the Pope claimed supremacy over the church, something that, with his Protestant historiographical perspective, was hardly coincidental, and revealed something of the infernal forces that lay behind both:

> Antichrist seems at this time to have set both his Feet upon Christendom together, the one in the East, the other in the West; and how much each has trampled upon the Church of Christ.[139]

Prideaux illustrates how the early modern English interpretations of Islam can not be easily disentangled from their rhetorical uses[140] (and Islam had been rhetorically useful for Christians of all persuasions, since its inception).[141] Despite Prideaux's protestations about the impartiality, accuracy and verifiability of the picture that he presents[142] the kind of 'knowledge' of Islam that his text demonstrates is self-serving and polemical.

The third text, Alexander Ross' *The Alcoran of Mahomet* (1649) is perhaps one that is even more signficant given the subject of this essay, as it represented the first time that the Qur'an had been rendered into English,[143] albeit not directly, but as a translation of André du Ryer's *L'Alcoran de Mahomet* which had been published a couple of years ear-

---

138 Prideaux 1697: xiv.

139 Prideaux 1697: 16.

140 A point well made by Pailin 1984: 105–136.

141 For example, at is crudest, 'early Protestants and their Catholic opponents yoked the Turks as God's *flagellum* and as agents of the Antichrist to their particular confessional agendas' (Colish 2009: 2), though some could have rather more sophisticated uses for the religion. See, for example, Bisaha 2006; Burman 2007; Campi 2010; Colish 2009; Elmarsafy 2009a, 2009b; Francisco 2007; Tolan 2002.

142 Prideaux 1697: iv–v.

143 Abraham Wheelock (1593–1653), Professor of Arabic in Cambridge, had attempted but failed to produce a Latin and Greek translation. There had been an earlier Latin translation by an Englishman, Robert of Ketton, in 1143, entitled *Lex Mahumet pseudoprophete* (see Burman 2007).

lier.[144] Ross' text seems to have been widely read, and two printings of the first edition were made. It remained the only version available until Sale's translation of 1734, which was undertaken in part because of Sale's horror at the incompetence of Ross. Sale complained that Ross' work was

> no more than a translation of Du Ryer's, and that a very bad one; for Alexander Ross, who did it being utterly unacquainted with the Arabic, and no great master of the French, has added a number of fresh mistakes of his own to those of Du Ryer; not to mention the meanness of his language, which would make a better book look ridiculous.[145]

Ross did not seek to endear his readers to the religious text he had 'translated'. The Qur'an was published with two appendices, 'The Life and Death of Mahomet' and 'A Needful Caveat', both of which maligned the prophet and the Qur'an, and were added in order to respond to the strong criticism that had greeted his first attempt to publish this work (the initial printing was seized following a petition to the Council of State).[146]

In the first appendix, Ross makes a number of attacks on the character of Muhammad and his revelation that are familiar from Christian anti-Muslim polemic: that Muhammad had received his creed from a disgruntled Nestorian Christian,[147] that Gabriel's revelation to Muhammad was in fact the result of epilepsy,[148] that he was a bandit leader,[149] that he used his prophecies to justify his own sexual appetite,[150] that he prophesied that he would rise from the dead after three days,[151] that he deliberately faked miracles to convince his followers.[152] The only positive thing that Ross says about Muhammad in his account is that: 'heaven ordained him to be a scourge for the punishment of Christians, who in

---

144 'Although it contains several serious mistakes, Du Ryer's translation was a vast improvement on what had gone before' (Elmarsafy 2009b: 8).
145 Sale 1734: vi.
146 Matar 1998b: 83.
147 Ross 1649: 396.
148 Ross 1649: 398.
149 Ross 1649: 400.
150 Ross 1649: 407.
151 Ross 1649: 404.
152 Ross 1649: 406.

multitudes at that time had foresaken the truth.'[153] In the second appendix, Ross seeks to reassure his readers that the text is not dangerous, with an array of arguments about the self-evident failings of the 'mishapen and deformed piece' that he has translated[154] (although it should be noted there are also some grudging admissions of its value: 'Aesop's Cock found a precious stone in a dunghill ... even so in the dirt of the Alcoran you shall finde some jewels of Christian virtues').[155]

Ross' *Alcoran* appeared a few months after the execution of Charles I, and Ross, a Royalist, High Anglican, attacked those Parliamentarian Puritans who had opposed its publication, claiming that they suffered from the same 'instability' of religion as the Turks. The 'Christian Reader', who Ross addresses in a preface to the work, is told not to fear its contents if they remain firm in the 'orthodox Religion' and keep themselves 'untainted' by the 'follies' of the Cromwellians, who 'having once abandoned the Sun of the Gospel, I believe they will wander as far into utter darkenesse, by following strange lights, as by this *Ignis Fatuus* of the Alcoran'.[156] Intra-Christian polemic emerges, once again, as a context within which Islam is presented in the anglophone world.

In all three cases the texts show the 'knowledge' of Islam that was current and dominant in early modern England, knowledge that had little to do with the living reality of the faith itself and the practices of its adherents. They are indicative of the prevalent view.

153 Ross 1649: 407.
154 Ross 1649: Ee2.
155 Ross 1649: Ee4.
156 Ross 1649: A3r.

6. Anglophone Anomalies

However, the picture presented, even if dominant, was not necessarily, quite what it seems. As Colley has noted, much language about Islam in English writing, accusations of despotism, superstition, backwardness, is similar to that used by the English of pretty much everyone who was not English. As she says: 'Then as now, the British possessed a durable and limited portmanteau of xenophobic language which they drew upon and deployed undiscriminantly.'[157] This language has its roots, she argues, in a combination of a sense of election and vulnerability. There were also, perhaps even more importantly, clear anomalies that disrupt the picture presented by Said and others, and so before we turn to the Quakers, it is useful to sketch something of these.

At a popular level there is evidence of a more positive reception of the cultures of early modern Islam than we might be led to expect. For example, the responses to the visit of the Moroccan ambassador Muhammad bin Hadu to England in 1681–1682 were striking not least in their judgement on his piety, intellect, manners and horsemanship – all of which were judged to put members of the English court and the ambassadors of other countries to shame.[158] He was even, amongst other things, warmly praised for having donated 15 guineas to the workmen erecting St Paul's in London.[159] The response is not so surprising when one notes, for example, the remarkable proliferation of coffee houses in England from the mid-1650s, in deliberate emulation of the Ottomans, and marketed to consumers in ways that assumed a positive estimation of Ottoman culture[160] – something possible, in part, as a consequence of the growth in trade with the Ottomans facilitated by the Levant Compa-

---

157 Colley 2002: 105.
158 See, for example, the diarist John Evelyn's remarks for January 24th 1682 (1907: 162). The famous portrait of Hadu riding his horse in Hyde Park by Godfrey Kneller and Jan Wyck, currently in Chiswick House, London, is indicative of this estimation of the ambassador.
159 Matar 2009: 103.
160 Rosee 1666.

ny.[161] The positive sentiments towards some Muslims can be seen in the records of charitable giving by parishes to assist destitute Moors liberated from enslavement by the success of the English navy, or Turks who had been shipwrecked in England, to pay for their passage home.[162] Such data is clearly at variance from the image derived from expressly anti-Islamic texts of Christian apologetics which have dominated many scholarly reconstructions.

Such a variegated view is also evident in the writings of some of the earliest Arabists in England, most notably, Edward Pococke, appointed the first Professor of Arabic at Oxford in 1636. Although interest in the Arabic language was primarily for the purpose of Biblical studies (Pococke was simultaneously Professor of Hebrew), nonetheless Pococke produced a remarkable translation and commentary on the work of the Syrian historian Bar Hebraeus in 1650[163] which, in rigorous and extensive footnotes, provided a largely impartial and well-documented account of the origins of Islam. A former chaplain of the Levant Company in Aleppo from 1630–1635,[164] Pococke remained in contact with Muslims throughout his subsequent academic life, and was also notable for convincing Hugo Grotius to allow some anti-Muhammad fables to be removed from Pococke's Arabic translation of his *De veritate religionis Christianae*, an extremely influential work of Christian apologetics. Pococke was a churchman and concerned with the propagation of his faith – for example, he translated the Anglican Book of Common Prayer into Arabic for missionary purposes – but his reception of Islam was clearly far more nuanced than most of his contemporaries.

It also had significant consequences. The work of Pococke became the basis of one of the most unusual texts of the period, Henry Stubbe's *An Account of the Rise and Progress of Mahometanism with the Life of Mahomet and a Vindication of Him and His Religion from the Calumnies of the*

---

161 Mather 2009. For the origins of the company see Eysturlid 1993.

162 St. Olave Jewry, for instance, gave 12d. to a 'moore taken by the turkes' (Guildhall Library [GL], MS 4409/1, f. 121). St. Lawrence Jewry helped 'foure poore Turkes undonn by sea.' (GL, MS 2593/1, f. 218v, 234; see also GL, MS 4457/2, f. 273v.). See Schen 2000: 461 and Matar 1997.

163 Pococke 1650.

164 For more on the role of Aleppo chaplains in the development of the study of Arabic in England, see Russell 1994: 40–45 and Mills 2011.

Christians,[165] which is a sustained piece of scholarship which effectively critiqued prevailing interpretations of the inception and development of Islam. It presents a strikingly positive picture of a gifted and virtuous Muhammad in conscious opposition to prevailing biographies of the time. For Stubbe, he

> was fuirnish'd with all the qualifications requisite in a person cut out for great Achievements and equally quallified for Actions of Warr, or the Arts of Peace and civil Government, which notwithstanding the Calumnies charged upon him by the Christians, will be evident to any one that will attentively consider the foregoing account of his Life and Actions, which I have extracted out of the best Authors, Arabians and others, but have justly rejected a great deal of the fabulous, ridiculous trash, with which most of the Christian Narrative of him are stuff'd.[166]

Stubbe's work is exceptional in the English language and, indeed, for seventeenth century Christian Europe. Stubbe undoubtedly harboured heterodox views[167] but the extensive, sustained treatment of Muhammad and Islam, and the level of detail evident in his argumentation, indicates that he was not primarily concerned with Islam for its rhetorical uses in attacking Christian orthodoxy (although the initial section of the book where he criticises prevailing assumptions about the origins of Christianity might indicate this); instead it is understanding and explaining Islam and Muhammad that is Stubbe's chief preoccupation. However, for all its novelty, Stubbe's text only circulated in manuscript form, and was not published until 1911, and so its influence was limited.

Perhaps unsurprisingly, literature produced by those early modern English who lived or regularly travelled in Muslim-majority lands, whether as diplomats, merchants, sailors, chaplains, or slaves, also provides us with a rich vein of anomalous pictures of Islam, which, unlike the picture pre-

---

165 For Stubbe see Birchwood 2007; Holt 1972; Jacob 1983.

166 Stubbe 1911: 142. The manuscript was originally written 1673–1676.

167 Early in his career he even wrote a work defending Quakers against their critics (Stubbe 1659).

sented by Stubbe, were published and had a popular currency.[168] Travel did not, of course, necessarily broaden the mind. For example, William Biddulph, the first English chaplain of the Levant Company to publish an account of his time in the Ottoman empire, wrote that Muhammad was an immoral agent of the devil who had established a fraudulent religion,[169] and declared that, after some years living in Aleppo, the only thing that had altered about him was the air that he breathed.[170] Nonetheless some accounts, presented a very different picture. For example, Sir Henry Blount travelled primarily to acquire knowledge about the Ottomans and also, to discern, in a Baconian, rational, and comparative manner, what this could tell him more generally about the age in which he lived. He was impressed by what he discovered, declaring that 'hee who would behold these times in their greatest glory, could find no better *Scene* than *Turky*'.[171]

Early modern travel narratives reveal constructions of the Orient that are far less homogeneous and predictable than the crude generalisations that have often been assumed to predominate. As Kenneth Parker has remarked, Britons encountering the Ottoman empire before the onset of 'Orientalism proper' appear, in fact, to have been 'dis-oriented', transfixed by the power and dominance of the Turks and their dominions.[172] Instead of reproducing the characteristics of fully-fledged Orientalism, literature of the early modern period, notably the much-studied travel narratives, 'recount cultural encounters in which self and other are not fixed in opposing positions but are rewritten through discursive and social interventions'.[173]

Indeed, amongst such travel writings, one is particularly significant. Joseph Pitts' *A faithfull account of the religion and manners of the Maho-*

168 The critical literature on early modern travel writing is extensive. See, for example, Kamps and Singh 2001; Carey and Jowitt 2009, 2012. For English travellers in the Ottoman empire see MacLean 2004; Mather 2009; Vitkus 2000.
169 Biddulph 1609: 46. Biddulph copied out word for word the polemical life of Muhammad found in the anonymous work *The Policy of the Turkish Empire* (1597). See MacLean 2004: 86.
170 Biddulph 1609: 32.
171 Blount 1636: 4. For Blount see MacLean 2004: 117–176.
172 Parker 1999: 3.
173 Kamps and Singh 2001: 3.

metans, in which is a particular relation of their pilgrimage to Mecca (1704) was written by a former English slave[174] who 'turn'd Turk' (converted to Islam), and then, whilst still a slave, accompanied his master on hajj.[175] The text he composed is particularly disruptive of the general presentations of Islam and Muslims in England in his day, and was quite self-consciously intended to be such. Although it deserves to be called a travel narrative, like many such accounts in early modern England, it is also one of travail and could be categorised as a captivity narrative,[176] and as with most captivity narratives of the time, it is an amalgam of a number of a genres, and contains extensive ethnographic description of the beliefs and practices of Muslims, of which, as Pitts claims in the title of his work, and numerous times within its text, he wishes to give a faithful account.

Although the subject of Pitts' work was unusual, the character of his work was not. As Pratt has demonstrated, in the early modern period a number of uneducated sailors authored books in which they described the practices and beliefs of people whom they encountered in a systematic, nuanced and impartial manner.[177] A comparable example would be Robert Knox's *An Historical Relation of the Island Ceylon in the East Indies* (1681) which details his capture, 19 years of captivity, and eventual escape, but also includes significant detail about the flora, fauna of Sri Lanka and ethnographic description of the culture of the inhabitants (although the religions he describes there are primarily Buddhism and Hinduism rather than Islam). Like modern ethnography such writers were not only keen to organise and structure their information in a clear and logical fashion but they also made an effort to be objective in their

---

174 Pitts was about fifteen when his fishing boat, the *Speedwell*, was captured by a corsair from Algiers off the coast of Spain in 1678 (the *Speedwell* is named in the list of boats lost to Barbary corsairs since 1677 that was published anonymously in London in 1682). He was a native of Exeter and was returning from Newfoundland when taken. He remained enslaved until 1685, but did not return home until 1694 (Auchterlonie 2012: 52–54). See also Beckingham 1950; Humberto 2011.

175 Another edition appeared in 1717, without his consent, and containing numerous errors, leading him to publish a third edition in 1731 and a further, expanded edition in 1738.

176 For an anthology of such accounts and a comprehensive list see Vitkus 2001: 371–376. See also Matar 2001b and Maclean and Matar 2011: 124–155 for useful introductions. There are a number of studies of the genre, but for captivity accounts in English see Snader 2000 and Benhayoun 2006.

177 Pratt 1986.

descriptions, even though they often wrote from an experience of enslavement. *The Captivity of Hans Stade of Hesse in A.D. 1547–1555, Among the Wild Tribes of Eastern Brazil*, in which Stade describes the manners of the Tupi Nambas people is typical of such works whose characteristics 'resemble those of modern ethnography in their specificity, their search for neutrality and even-handedness, and their linkage of social and material order.'[178] However, unlike modern ethnography, or some of their more educated peers, such writers did not, for example, look back to the likes of Herodotus nor stand self-consciously in a tradition of academic practice; theirs could be said to be ethnology without erudition.

However, Pitts' motivation for writing his account was somewhat different from the likes of Stade or Knox. Pitts was keen to correct misinformation about Muhammad and Islam in general, and as someone who was unique in England for having actually *seen* Mecca, he felt well placed to do so.[179] Although he is reticent about naming names, he makes it clear that his account is intended to correct 'Mistakes in Authors, who are persons of great Learning and Worth'.[180] He pointedly rejects, for example, the legend that Muhammad used a trained pigeon to pick grain out of his ear to give the appearance that he was being inspired by the Holy Ghost,[181] a medieval fable that Ross had included in his *Alcoran*,[182] and he also ridiculed the idea that Muhammad's tomb was suspended in the air by virtue of magnets, another common fable.[183] Pitts does still use language typical of early modern English Protestants in his evaluation of Islam,[184] and he can even make a favourable reference in one footnote to the work of Prideaux,[185] but on the whole, as its subsequent impact upon Sale and others testifies,[186] Pitts' work achieves it purpose, providing an

178 Pratt 1986: 34.
179 Pitts 1731: viii.
180 Pitts 1731: viii.
181 Pitts 1731: x.
182 Ross 1649: 406.
183 Pitts 1731: 10. For the definitive treatment of the origin of this tradition see Eckhardt 1949. See also Akbari 2009: 232–234.
184 See, for example, 1731: 43 where Pitts describes the Qur'an as 'that Legend of Falsities, and abominable Follies and Absurdities'.
185 Pitts 1731: 18.
186 Sale references Pitts in the forward to his 1734 edition of the Qur'an, when refuting the common myth that Muhammad's tomb in Mecca was suspended in the air

impressive record of the religion as encountered, rather than a fabricated construction, assembled from the detritus of medieval legend and tropes of contemporary polemic.

Publishing such an account was not unproblematic. Pitts' text is dominated by the fact that he had 'turn'd Turk' whilst a slave, making him a 'renegade', a transgressive, and largely despised figure in European cultures,[187] a figure whose religious identity was often judged unstable and whose testimony was deemed untrustworthy.[188] It is no surprise, therefore, that he felt compelled to justify his apostasy, and Pitts devotes a considerable part of his account to explaining how he was coerced into converting,[189] suffering tortures and abuse (although he notes that this was actually very unusual) and that he was filled with remorse,[190] always retaining 'a Christian heart'.[191] Pitts makes references to those who clearly doubted whether he really had no choice but to convert and questioned why he stayed so long in the Ottoman empire when a free man (and by implication, the sincerity of his return to his Christian faith). In his defence he makes a telling remark about the acknowledged lure of life in Ottoman lands, which for many, especially poor Europeans, could be viewed as a place of wealth and opportunity, asking them to consider

---

by the use of magnets (the tomb is, in any case, in Medina, as Pitts was at pains to inform his readers). Interestingly Prideaux also rejected this (1697: 134), as well as the common claim that Muhammad had trained a pigeon to appear to whisper in his ear, as though it were the Holy Spirit (1697: 48; see Mark 1:10).

187 See Matar 1993; Burton 2005. Although sometimes they viewed rather more romantically in popular culture, as poor men made good, as can be seen in the ambivalence of representations of, for example, Jack Ward (also known by his Muslim name of Yusuf Reis) who became the leader of the corsairs of Tunis in the early 1600s. See Matar 1998a: 57; Tinniswood 2010: 14–45. For important studies of renegades in the early modern Mediterranean see Dursteler 2011 and Bennassar and Bennassar 2006.

188 Somewhat paradoxically, Pitts declares that his account should be trusted because if he did not speak the truth, it would be a 'bad testimony of my repentance for my apostasy' (Pitts 1731: viii).

189 See, for example, Pitts 1731: chapter ix.

190 See, for example, his exchange of letters with his father (Pitts 1731: 201). Interestingly ministers in England advised his father to take a more lenient position in his judgement of his son's apostasy.

191 Pitts 1731: xviii, 194. This is a common trope in such accounts. See Pellow 1739.

'what hazard I ran in making my escape. I was in a much fairer way for honour and preferment in Algier, than I could expect ever in England.'[192]

Having outlined something of the distinctive character of early Quakerism, the nature of Barbary slavery, and early modern English representations of Islam, providing a necessary context for our study, let us now turn to Quaker slaves in Barbary and the images of Islam that were generated by their experience.

---

192 Pitts 1731: xvii.

7. Quaker Slaves

The phenomenon of Quaker slaves should not come as a surprise to anyone familiar with early Quaker literature. All editions of George Fox's *Epistles*, from their initial publication in 1698, have included those letters written by him to Quaker slaves in Barbary. Indeed, the final epistle in the collection, dated 25th of 8th Month 1690, and written a few weeks before his death, is addressed 'To Friends, Captives at Macqueness' (Meknes, Morocco).[193] Nonetheless, aside from two articles on Quaker slaves in Algiers and Morocco by Kenneth Carroll,[194] little has been written about this phenomenon, and the existence of Quaker slaves has largely been passed over by those who study the early years of this movement and its encounter with Islam.[195]

Perhaps one of the reasons this phenomenon has been ignored is that the term 'slavery' for the experience of Quaker captives in North Africa might seem an inappropriate one that implies a homogeneity of experience between these Quakers (and other Barbary slaves) and those slaves of African origin who were transported to the West Indies and the Americas.[196] Some scholars question whether Barbary slavery constituted real 'slavery'; after all, those enslaved were often referred to as 'captives', as we can see in the title of Fox's final letter,[197] and although Barbary slaves were

---

193 Fox 1698: 557 (Ep. 420).

194 Carroll 1982 and 1985–1986.

195 Vlasblom, despite discussing Quakers, Islam and slavery (2011: 14–15) shows no awareness of the existence of actual Quaker slaves. See, though, Tuke 1848.

196 See, for example, Schwarz 2008: 74. As Davis has noted, the Mediterranean experience has been inexorably entwined with evaluations of the North Atlantic slave trade, and American and British complicity in its horrors has made it something that is a particularly difficult subject to examine (Davis 2003: xxvi).

197 This is something of a red-herring as the term 'captive' and 'slave' were synonyms at the time. Although the Quaker slaves could refer to themselves as 'captives', as did Fox and other Friends when writing to or about them, and the collection set up in 1678 to support and redeem the Quakers in Barbary was entitled 'The Redemption of Captives Fund', this term was not one that distinguished them from 'slaves'. For example, Fox himself speaks of the Quaker captives as slaves in his letter *To the Great Turk and his King, at Argiers* published in 1680, in which he pleaded for their

sold in slave markets, like the victims of the Atlantic slave trade, the former, or at least some of them, had the possibility of being redeemed from slavery, something virtually unknown in the experience of Atlantic slavery.[198] But whilst there were significant differences, and Atlantic slavery was judged by some contemporaries to be more harsh in comparison with that in Barbary,[199] at its heart Barbary slavery did consist of the ownership of one human being by another, a basic characteristic of slavery, and some of the differences should not be exaggerated – relative to the total captured, few slaves were redeemed[200] or survived long in Barbary.[201]

better treatment, and the Epistles of London Yearly Meeting refer to the condition of the Quakers as 'slavery'. See, for example, Yearly Meeting Epistle 4th Month 3rd 1691 (Friends House, London).

198 See Al-Ahari 2006: 12–14; Bluet 1734.

199 For example, the 1678 reprint of Richard Blome's *A Description of the Island of Jamaica*, first published in 1672, included a further tract as an appendix entitled 'together with the present state of Algiers'. In this addition to his original text Blome contrasted North Atlantic slavery with that of slavery in Algiers (Blome 1678: 7). The Quaker George Keith used this in one of his arguments against the validity of Christians owning slaves in his 1693 work, *An exhortation & caution to friends concerning buying and keeping of negroes*. In his fourth proposition, he complains that some Christian slave owners make 'far worse usage' of their slaves 'than is practised by the Turks and Moors upon their Slaves' which 'tends to the great Reproach of the Christian Profession' (Keith 1693: 5). It will not only lead to the slave owners' punishment by God but allows infidels to 'blaspheme the Blessed Name of Christ'. (Keith 1693: 5).

200 Those without wealth or status, which was virtually all of those captured, considered redemption unlikely. Coxere, for example, remarks that on his capture he was particularly despondent because he did not have the resources to have himself redeemed 'and knew not but that I might a ended my days a slave under the hands of merciless men' (Coxere in Meyerstein 1945: 54). Coxere's brother-in-law had contacts with merchants in Livorno and so he was released after only two months' captivity on the payment of 'eight hundred pieces of eight' (Meyerstein 1945: 57). For those enslaved in the last quarter of the seventeenth century 'there was no Hope of being redeemed' (Braithwaite 1729: 150). This was particularly true of Morocco, and especially after 1682 when the emperor Moulay Ismail issued a decree that abolished private ownership of slaves in his kingdom.

Protestant slaves were less likely to be redeemed than Catholics as they did not benefit from the regular, if limited, redemptions negotiated by Redemptionist orders (Matar 2001b: 29) and, aside from occasional redemptions organised by their governments; or, on occasion, local officials, they were left to their own devices. In England, for example, although licenses were issued by Trinity House for raising funds to redeem captives (Matar 2001b: 24-25), action by the state was regularly criticised as ineffectual (see, for example, Brooks 1693: xix). Most redemptions by the English seem to have been haphazard, unpredictable affairs (see, for example, Digby 1868: 15–19 [1628]).

201 The brutality many slaves experienced at the hands of their owners, and the conditions they endured as slaves (which often included deprivation, exposure, injury

Let us begin by sketching something of the experience of Barbary slavery of the Quakers. Sufficient numbers of Friends were captured by Barbary corsairs to form an identifiable group of about twenty in Algiers by 1675 when they are first mentioned in George Fox's epistle *To Friends in Barbadoes*.[202] As the last of the slaves remaining alive in Algiers obtained their freedom in 1688, groups of Quaker slaves appeared in Morocco at the port of Sally (Salé) just north of Rabat, and also Meknes, the capital and showpiece of Moulay Ismail's kingdom, some eighty miles to the south-east. The Moroccan Quakers would continue to exist as an identifiable group, a 'Meeting' in Quaker terminology, until 1701 when the last of those that were still left alive were redeemed.[203] Their numbers were comparable to the group that had been enslaved in Algiers. These Quakers were mostly English speaking and came from England, Ireland, North America, and the West Indies, although they also included a Quaker, Gerard Serrenson, from Norway.[204]

There was a group of Quaker slaves at Murbay[205] too who had correspondence with the Quakers enslaved in Morocco in the early 1691.[206] However, we know little about this Meeting and even its geographical location is uncertain. 'Murbay' is described as being 'three or four days 'journey distant' from Meknes,[207] but it has proved impossible to determine where exactly this might be, and other than that the Meeting consisted of a handful of slaves who had converted to Quakerism, we know little more. Soon after reporting that one of their number had been killed

---

and disease) led to high rates of mortality amongst those in Barbary. We know, for example, that of the Icelanders captured in 1627, who were fortunate to end up in Algiers, regarded as somewhat better than other Barbary ports such Salé, less than 20% were still alive eight years later (Helgason 1997: 276).

202 Fox 1698: 354 (Ep. 315). Contra Carroll 1982: 302, who does not seem aware of the evidence in this epistle and dates the inception of this group some years later, to 1679. We may have earlier evidence of Quaker enslavement, although the information is rather equivocal (see Mortimer 1971: 93).

203 Of the Quakers enslaved in Morocco, about half died in captivity, and those finally redeemed had been slaves for an average of 17 years each (Tuke 1848: 22).

204 See Carroll 1982 and 1987.

205 Epistle of Yearly Meeting 1691 (London Yearly Meeting 1858: 1.57).

206 Epistle of Yearly Meeting 1691 (London Yearly Meeting 1858: 1.57).

207 For the brief references to this Murbay group see Carroll 1987: 73; Tuke 1848: 13, 16.

in 1692 they disappear from our records, their fate, like so many who were enslaved in Barbary, unknown and unknowable.

From our records it is clear that the majority of Quakers who were enslaved were, like most of the English captured by Barbary corsairs, sailors of various kinds, including captains, such as Henry Tregnoe, Joseph Wasey and Daniel Baker, as well as assorted crew members, such as Richard Udy, a ship's carpenter, and Bartholomew Cole, a boatswain, and Gerard Serrenson, John King, Thomas Walkenden, and Robert Finley, plain seamen.[208] A few are described as having a trade – Richard Robinson is described as a leather-dresser and Ephraim Gilbert as a cooper, and some seem to have been merchants, such as John Harbin.[209] Anyone travelling by sea was a potential victim of the corsairs and whilst this was particularly true of those trading in the Mediterranean, it could occur anywhere. For example, in 1679, the king's appointment as governor of Carolina, Seth Sothell, was captured crossing the Atlantic to take up his post,[210] Jeffrey Hudson ('Lord Minimus'), a favourite of Queen Henrietta Maria, met a similar fate, whilst crossing the English Channel in 1644,[211] the Reverend Devereux Spratt, who later became famous for voluntarily staying in Algiers for sometime after his redemption in order to look after his co-religionists, was initially seized crossing the Irish sea.[212] George Fox

---

208 For details of individuals see Carroll 1982, 1985–1986. Indeed, Quaker captains could be more likely to be captured than others because their refusal to swear oaths of any kind meant that they were unable to obtain a pass that could, from time to time, depending upon the status of treaties between England and the various Barbary states, allow safe passage for their ships. In 1677, for example, the Quaker captain Thomas Hutson, his crew, and ship, the *Patience*, languished, albeit briefly, in Algiers for this reason even though England and the Dey of Algiers were, at the time, at peace (Waysblum 1959: 110; see also Coxere 1945: 108).

209 See Carroll 1985-86: 77. The Harbin enslaved in Morocco was probably John, the son of Joseph Harbin, a successful Quaker merchant on Barbados (Gragg 2009: 68, 76, 95). Joseph's will refers to a son currently enslaved in Salé (New England Historic Genealogical Society 1984: 716), and John Harbin reappeared in Barbados in 1693 (Rawlins 1951), evidence of his redemption. John is confused with his father or brother in the Yearly Meeting Epistle of 1687, one of the records that refers to a Harbing or Harbin in Morocco, and this has led to some uncertainty about his fate (Carroll 1985–86: 69, 78).

210 See Riddell 1930.

211 Page 2001: 190. See also Wright 1684: 105.

212 See Spratt 1886.

himself was nearly enslaved in 1671 whilst making his way to Barbados.[213] The possibility of being captured was such a commonplace that it is unsurprising that the eponymous Robinson Crusoe's first misfortune, in one of the earliest English novels, is to be captured by a ship from Salé and enslaved there for two years.[214] On occasion some English people could be taken directly from coastal settlements. For example, in one month alone in 1646, 'seven barbary ships' carried off 'goods and prisoners including about two hundred women' from Cornwall[215] – although this was rare compared with the scale of depredations suffered by other nations, especially those who had populations living on the Mediterranean coast.[216] However, by far the greatest number of victims amongst the English were sailors or fishermen and the Quaker slaves reflected this.[217] There is no evidence of any more than a handful of Quakers being captured at any one time, and despite some close scrapes – a party of German Quaker colonists travelling to Pennsylvania were nearly seized in 1683[218] – we never hear of any boats containing Quaker colonists falling victim to corsairs.[219]

The Quaker slaves were not all Quakers when captured by privateers. A number, to use the Quaker terminology of the day, were 'convinced' subsequent to their capture. For some this was the result of having come

---

213 Penney 1911: 2.181–182, 215, 437. He gave thanks for being saved from 'pirates and robbers' in a letter to his wife, Margaret Fell, upon his return in 1673. See Cadbury 1972: 109.

214 Defoe 1719: 19.

215 Matar 2001a: 252.

216 In Friedman's study of Spanish captives in Barbary she determined that one fifth of all those enslaved had been taken from land rather than sea. See Friedman 1983: 4.

217 See, for example, Anon. 1682.

218 This is referred to in a letter by Francis Daniel Pastorius, one of the founders of Germantown (see Myers 1912: 392). The ship, the *America*, was captained by the Quaker Joseph Wasey, who would subsequently be captured.

219 Matar appears to claim this (1999: 116) but the text to which he refers, *The Case of Many Hundreds of Poor English Captives* (1680), is not one that mentions Quakers nor has any direct association with Friends. However, he is right that the abuse that this text details may have provoked Fox's 1680 tract *To the Great Turk* (see Matar 1989: 272).

Colonists were regularly captured by corsairs. William Okeley, for example, was taken whilst on his way to a new Puritan colony in the Caribbean (Providence Island). He was a slave from 1639 but escaped to Majorca with four others in 1644 in a secretly constructed boat. His captivity account, first published in 1675, is a pious, Puritan version of a popular genre, combining edification with derring-do (Snader 2000).

into contact with Quaker slaves, as their convincement took place after the establishment of a Meeting, something that was the case with Richard Robinson, one of the final group to be freed from Morocco.[220] However, a few declared themselves to be Quakers after their enslavement though before any formal contact with Friends.[221]

The reports that came back to Quakers in England about the fate of their co-religionists are unsurprising to anyone familiar with the literature of Barbary slavery more generally. They emphasised the extreme deprivation and regular violence experienced by most of the enslaved.[222] So, for example, Ephraim Gilbert, from Bermuda, complained in a letter that he was 'pretty hardly used by stripes and fetters of iron' and for one period, kept for two weeks chained in a cellar to two sheep, on a diet of bread and water before being beaten on the soles of his feet with a pizzle – a dried bull's penis (a regular form of punishment and torture in the Barbary states).[223]

Sometimes this abuse had a specifically religious aspect to it. In 1680, for example, John Clagget was reported as having been 'used very severely' and received '20 stripes together and that most days to make him turn Moare'.[224] Such behaviour was counter to normal practice by Muslim masters in Barbary and went against Quaker expectations of Turks.[225] Stephen Smith, for example, a Quaker who had, before his conversion,

---

220 Tuke 1848: 22.

221 See, for example, Arthur Wastcoat and James Burgin. Meeting for Sufferings Minutes (Friends House, London) [MfS] 5: 357; 6: 46; see Carroll 1985–1986: 69. This is not quite as unusual as it might appear as we have accounts of 'convincements' that occurred some time after any contact with Quakers or exposure to Quaker ideas. Lurting, for example, tells us of two sailors who declared themselves Quakers some six months after speaking to a Quaker, the first sign of their new faith being their refusal to hear a priest or take off their hats to their captain (Lurting 1710: 10).

222 There were though exceptions. Francis Jackson, redeemed in 1685, reported that he had been able to work as a milliner whilst enslaved and had received no more then ten blows during the whole period of his enslavement. Carroll 1982: 311. MfS 4: 150.

223 Carroll 1982: 309; MfS 4: 98. In the case of Gilbert and many others, this violence had a very specific economic purpose – to increase the ransom price demanded for a slave. A slave would be forced to agree to a much higher price for his freedom if his experience was unendurable. Indeed, Gilbert claims that this is why he endured these punishments and why he was put to work carrying heavy stones rather than being allowed to practise his trade as a cooper.

224 Carroll 1982: 304. MfS 1: 144.

225 See, for example, Fox 1677: 10.

been employed for some years by the Levant Company in Alexandretta (Iskenderun), the port of Aleppo, made much of the Turks' reticence at gaining converts for the wrong reasons, by either threat or favour, when describing their behaviour in his work *Wholsome Advice [sic]* – a work in which he compared the behaviour of Muslims with that of non-Quaker Christians, to the detriment of the latter.[226]

In one case, that of Bartholomew Cole, a convert to Quakerism from Islam, the threat of religiously motivated violence was particularly dangerous. Cole was the boatswain of the *Kent*, a ship captained by another Quaker, Henry Tregony, when it was captured by corsairs operating out of Algiers in 1678. We learn of his original faith in a letter sent to Meeting for Sufferings, the national body set up by Quakers only a few years earlier to support Friends enduring persecution, which requested that it advance funds for his redemption as soon as possible. The letter informed the committee that Cole's plight was particularly pressing as he 'was born a Turke and if it be known that he is turned Christian from being a Mahometan by the Custome of the country he is not to be Ransomed but burnt.'[227] He was fortunate to be redeemed very swiftly in late 1679,[228] before his status was discovered, probably suffering only about fourteen months enslavement.[229]

A number of the reports that reached Meeting for Sufferings also stressed the sexual violence of some of the captors towards those enslaved, particularly young men. For example, in 1680 it was reported that the Quaker 'lad' James Braynes had fallen 'into the hands of a beastly Patrone, who because he will not prostrate his body to his cursed will, hath (as we are credibly informed) beat him 2 or 3000 Blows & more. Such Cruel things he hath and (as far as we know) doth yet suffer.'[230] Similar remarks were made about Francis Cooley, although in his case, he was

---

226 See Smith 1676 (reprint in Smith 1679: 159-160). See also Fox 1677: 9–10; Fox 1673: 164.

227 MfS 1: 109 (3.5.1679). Being burnt alive as a punishment for apostasy appears in a number of Barbary captivity accounts. See, for example, D'Aranda 1666: 200.

228 MfS 1: 129 (4.10.1679).

229 It is clear from the list of ships taken by corsairs published in 1682 that most of the crew were still in Algiers some three years later (Anon. 1682: 2).

230 Carroll 1982: 304. MfS 1: 148.

murdered in late 1681 resisting rape.[231] Such sexual violence was referred to in most travel or captivity accounts of Barbary in this period.[232] Whilst not denying the suffering of some slaves, accusations of sodomy and related activities were part of the repertoire of alterity that could be deployed in early modern English culture. It is no surprise that such behaviour was regularly ascribed to Turks[233] although it was also an accusation that was made against any despised group in order to emphasise their reprehensible difference; it was common, for example, in representations of Jews[234] and Native Americans too.[235] Indeed, Quakers were accused of bestiality, an activity regarded as a comparable vice by most in the period.[236]

However, the suffering of the Quakers in Algiers was compounded by their distinctive practices, notably their refusal to give 'hat-honour', to remove their hat in the presence of social superiors. This was one of a number of forms of behaviour that marked Quakers out as a group distinct from other Christians and which they expended considerable energies defending[237] (indeed, in the year 1655 alone eight tracts were authored by Quakers to this end).[238] The refusal to give hat-honour had a number of motivations. It was intended to signify both that God and Christ are no 'respecter of persons',[239] and also that Quakers, unlike other Christians, avoided the trap of 'serving and bowing and worshiping the Creature more than the Creator'.[240] It was related to other distinctive practices, notably Quakers' use of plain language, and their refusal to em-

---

231 Carroll 1982: 308. MfS 2: 70.

232 Anon. 1680: 1.

233 Matar 1999: 109–127. Resistance to sodomy, to the point of death, became part of European representations of Barbary and viewed as a form of martyrdom. See, for example, Anon. 1676.

234 Webster 2006.

235 Matar 1999:109–127. It was also associated with pirates. See Turley 1999.

236 Denham 1659; Gilpin 1655: 20; see Leviticus 18:22–23.

237 Bitterman 1973. Some other, short-lived, radical religious groups that emerged in the English Revolution did also practise this. The Fifth Monarchy Men, for example, also refused to give hat-honour (Capp 1972: 143).

238 Moore 2000: 120.

239 Romans 2:11; Acts 10:34; James 2:1.

240 Fox 1656: 4.

ploy greetings,[241] honorific pronouns[242] or titles. These practices not only distinguished Quakers in their own mind from everyone else, whatever their creed or status, who followed the 'world's customs' and lived in 'darkness',[243] but also formed part of their 'rhetoric of impoliteness', behaviours which challenged not so 'much religious or political institutions as the very fabric of social relations and social inter-action'.[244] Refusal to pay 'hat honour' was not something negotiable in the eyes of Quakers as it went to the heart of their understanding of the gospel. As Fox put it:

> Now putting off the hat is but a custome got up amongst the Christians (and fining for not doing it) since the Apostles in the Apostacie, a vain custome, set up by Traditions, which is a worship of men, and of the beast, and honour below, and an Idol set up by transgressors.[245]

Quakers were aware that the cultural significance of baring one's head was greater in European countries than in the Barbary states or the Ottoman empire – and often drew attention to this in their criticisms of other Christians. Fox, for example, noted that 'the Turks mock at the Christians and say they spend most of their time in shewing their bare heads one to another',[246] and Stephen Smith remarked that it was 'a Cause of Laughter unto them [the Turks] to see the Christians...Scraping with the Leg, and Daughing the Hat and Foolish Gestures'.[247] Nonetheless, observing this distinctive practice had consequences amongst the Quakers in Barbary. Refusing hat-honour could still appear insulting and insubordinate, particularly when it came from a slave and it resulted in at least one Quaker, Joseph Todderdell, being beaten and eventually killed by his owner in Algiers in 1685.[248] And it seems from the text of one of Fox's epistles writ-

---

241 See, for example, Fox 1657 or Furly 1663.
242 For early Quakers the use of the second person plural to address a single person was unacceptable and a sign of social deference.
243 Fox 1657.
244 Bauman 1984: 43.
245 Fox 1657: 25.
246 Cadbury 1972: 25.
247 Smith 1676: 6 (1679: 164).
248 In Morocco we also hear that the emperor Moulay Ismail considered the refusal of Christian slaves to remove their hats in his presence as a grave insult. According to

ten to the Algiers Quakers, the strong reaction this Quaker practice could provoke from owners was not limited only to the master of Todderdell.[249]

The kind of offence that Quakers might give by adhering to the 'rhetoric of impoliteness'[250] in the context of early modern North African Muslim culture is seen in the words of Isuf Chaous, a wealthy Ottoman convert to English Puritanism, baptised in London 1658. According to a report of his conversion, albeit provided by Thomas White, a Puritan, the Turk, on making his way to England to seek out Protestants having been disappointed with experience of Catholicism in France, encountered some Quakers

> who came to him with their hands in their pockets, and using those rude carriages which they are known to use to all, though of never so great quality: withal telling him that we should not use any titles of honor or civilities to any. He told me he was much offended at their demeanour, and said unto them that for his part, that he thought that Worship was due to God and Courtesie to man.[251]

Given the violence experienced by many enslaved Friends, it is perhaps unsurprising that some of those who were eventually redeemed from their enslavement in Barbary had nothing positive to say about their captors. Levin Bufkin, for example, redeemed in January 1680, wrote expressing his gratitude to a Friend with these words:

> I am Redeemed out of Captivity I suppose by order of thee and other friends, which Deliverance is never to bee forgotten by mee for which my soul hath Cause to bless the Lord who hath Delivered mee from the soard and from the pestelence and from the Rage of Cruell faithless and blodyminded men and hath been a presant helpe and a staye to mee in time of need, blessed bee his name for Ever moare.[252]

Busnot, he killed a Spanish slave who crossed his path whilst carrying water and failed to remove his hat (1715: 151).

249 Fox 1698: 503 (Ep. 391, [1684]).

250 Bauman 1983: 43.

251 White and Drury 1659: xviii.

252 Carroll 1982: 312.

8. Paradoxes

However, there was much that was paradoxical about the experience of the early Quakers in North Africa. Quakers had endured persecution, both at home and abroad, since the inception of the movement. This took the form of specific legislation aimed at Quakers and other dissenters, such as the Quaker Act of 1662 and the Conventicle Acts of 1664 and 1670, that effectively outlawed Quaker worship, but they also suffered prosecution under laws that were of a more general kind, such as the Blasphemy Act of 1650 and the Elizabethan Vagrancy Acts which were regularly used against itinerant Quaker women and men.[253] The legal consequences of various non-negotiable principles also inevitably led them into conflict with the forces of the established church and the state, such as their refusal to pay church tithes or swear oaths.[254] The consequences of any legal proceedings became all the greater because:

> Friends refused to enter into bail, to give sureties for good behaviour or to appear in court, because they would not admit to having done anything wrong, nor would they pay court fees when summoned to answer what they regarded as unfounded accusations, or jail fees after what they saw as unmerited imprisonments.[255]

In addition, Quakers also regularly suffered malicious prosecutions, including accusations of magic. For example, in 1659, Cambridge Quakers were brought to trial accused of bewitching a woman and changing her into a horse.[256] Violence from neighbours and others hostile to their provocative claims and stubborn behaviour was also endemic. The refusal of members to physically defend themselves seems to have only increased

---

253 See Coffey 2000: 151–155; 166–179.
254 See Ayoub 2005; Horle 1988.
255 Miller 2005: 71.
256 Anon. 1659. See Elmer 1996; Gummere 1908: 30–35.

the violence meted out.[257] *Ad hoc* persecutions reached their zenith in the 1650s, but other forms of persecution continued throughout the seventeenth century, long after the Act of Toleration in 1689 that relieved many of the legal restrictions upon them and other Protestant sectaries (though not the Unitarians). At times the intensity of the persecution was significant with more than 15,000 Quakers imprisoned, or otherwise punished, between 1663–1689.[258] About four hundred and fifty died as a direct result of their treatment.[259]

And, paradoxically, Friends were freer to practise their religion as slaves in Barbary than they were in England,[260] as we can see from the first reference to their captivity, an epistle of Fox to Quakers in Barbados in 1675. The brief section in the epistle where he touches on this is worth quoting in full:

> At Algier in the Turks Country Friends there have set up a Meeting amongst themselves (which are Captives) about Twenty Friends, and some other of the Captives have been Convinced at that Meeting.

> And one Thomas Tilby, a Captive Friend, hath a Testimony for God, and speaks there among them; and their Patroons, or Masters, let them meet; and one of their Masters spoke to a Friend, as he was going to a Meeting, and thought he had been going to a publick Tipling House, and he stop'd him, and ask'd him where he was going, and he told him, to Worship the Great God;

---

257 See Miller 2005.

258 Braithwaite 1955: 115.

259 Braithwaite 1995: 115. Braithwaite's figures are approximations based on the indexes of Besse (1753).

260 The situation of Friends in the English colonies varied greatly as some of the colonies had considerable autonomy in the development of their own laws and distinctive religious identities that were more or less accommodating towards Friends. The Puritan authorities in Massachusetts, for example, outdid England by executing Quakers, a practice that was only stopped by the direct intervention of Charles II. They then instituted the Cart and Whip Act of 1661 which required that Quakers be whipped out of the colony. Other punishments such as branding, ear cropping and imprisonment were common (Ryan 2009: 40). However, some colonies, from the outset, were more tolerant, notably Rhode Island. From 1674 the situation changed considerably as Quakers obtained three colonies of their own, West Jersey, Delaware, and Pennsylvania, and substantial immigration took place (Fischer 1989: 419–603), driven, in part, by the persecution in England.

and he said, it was well, and let him go; and some of the Turks said, They had some among them of their People, that would not buy Stolen Goods: I have written a large Epistle to encourage them, and that they might Preach the Gospel abroad in those Parts, both in their Words, Lives, and Conversations; and this Meeting there, among the Turks, may be of great service.[261]

It is telling that Fox's report that Quakers in Algiers had the freedom to establish a 'Meeting' appears immediately *after* he had informed the Quakers in Barbados that 'great persecution are in most counties in England, and many are imprisoned in many places, and their goods spoiled'.[262] 1675 was indeed a very hard year for English Friends and earlier that year Fox himself had been released from fourteen months of imprisonment in Worcester; it was the year that Friends felt the need to establish the Meeting for Sufferings, to provide institutional support for those being persecuted.[263] In a letter in 1683 Fox would repeat this point to the Quaker captives in Algiers themselves, saying 'I think you have more liberty to meet there than we have here; for they keep us out of our meetings, and cast us into prison, and spoil our goods'.[264]

Before Fox was faced with this evidence, he had already shown some awareness of the relative religious freedom found in Ottoman lands, something well known amongst his contemporaries.[265] Some fifteen years earlier he had used the fact that the Turks allowed Christians and Jews to worship freely to criticise those Christians who restricted Quakers from so doing. For example, in 1660, in his work *Concerning Christ Jesus the Covenant of God*, he stated: 'And in Turkey, paying tributes, people may have their liberty to worship their God ... though we paying our taxes, are plucked out by the hair of the head, from prayer out of our houses, and not suffered to pray together; as the heathen would.'[266] Although,

---

261 Fox 1698: 354 (Ep. 315).
262 Fox 1698: 353 (Ep. 315).
263 Ingle 1994: 267.
264 Fox 1698: 493 (Ep. 388 [1683]).
265 Birchwood 2005: 65–66; MacLean and Matar 2011: 165–167. The Mughals also had this reputation. See Sapra 85–88.
266 Fox 1706: 224 [1660]; also in Fox 1831 IV: 268. A similar view is found in a private epistle to Margaret Fell in the same year, in which he asked her to petition the newly restored king to allow religious freedom and noted that in failing to persecute reli-

from this text, it is clear that Fox was aware of the *jizyah* (tribute), which was levied upon non-Muslim subjects to allow them this freedom, it is contrasted favourably by him with the lack of freedom that Quakers experienced despite paying of taxes (other than church tithes) in England. The relative freedom of Christians in Ottoman lands was likewise used by him in his response to the Conventicle Act of 1664, one of the laws that effectively made Quaker worship illegal. In his tract he went to some lengths to describe religious liberty under the Turks in attacking the repressive consequences of this legislation.[267]

However, the actual experience of the Quakers, particularly in Algiers (Quakers could worship in Morocco but under much harsher conditions)[268] gave Fox a concrete example with which to shame Christian authorities who prevented Quakers from meeting and it was something he returned to on a number of occasions. So, for example, in his 1684 epistle *To The Chief Magistrates, Rulers, Ministers, Justices Of The Peace, And Other Officers* he contrasted the persecutions carried out by Christians with the practice of the Turks who:

> when they conquer any nation or people, or take captives, we do not hear that they force them to their religion. For our Friends, (the people called Quakers,) in Algiers, that are taken captives by the Turks, have their liberty peaceably to meet together, to serve and worship God there without disturbance.[269]

And in 1689 he wrote something similar to the magistrates of Dantzick who were persecuting Quakers in their jurisdiction.

---

gious dissenters 'Turks outstrip Christians that do profess Christ Jesus'. See Cadbury 1939: 75 (Ep. 127d [1660]).

267 Fox 1706; 305–306 (1668). See also Fox 1831 IV: 359–360. This was written in response to the *Conventicle Act* of 1664.

268 Carroll 1987: 73. Epistle of Yearly Meeting 1691 (Society of Friends 1858: 1.57). Quakers had to gather at night.

269 Fox 1706: 927 (1684), See also Fox 1831 VI: 274.

> Are not you worse than the Turks, who let many religions be in their country, yea, Christians, and to meet peaceably? Yea, the Turkish patroons let our friends that were captives meet together at Algiers, and said, "It was good so to do". You are worse than those barbarous people at Salee, who do not profess Christianity?[270]

The freedom of worship enjoyed by the Quaker slaves was not unique[271] but it was much valued and a constituent part of the image of Islam that emerges from Quaker writings. Indeed, Edward Coxere, a Quaker who, before his 'convincement', was enslaved in Porto Farina, Tunis,[272] and wrote a detailed account of his sufferings there, illustrated with his own drawings of chained slaves being whipped by their Barbary owners, complained, when imprisoned with seven other Quakers in Yarmouth, England, some years later, that[273]

> such unkind usage I never had when I was a slave under the hands of the Turks, such as the Christians call Infidels, that though I was chained a-nights with a great iron chain, and was made to work a-days, and sometimes beat, yet they gave me a bellyful of bread to eat with my water; but here, among my countrymen and such as called Christians, they gave me not the privilege as they gave their dogs.[274]

---

270 Fox 1694: 596 (1689). See also Fox 1831 II: 345–346.

271 See, for example, the conventicle of Protestants in Algiers mentioned in Okeley 1684, and led by the Reverend Devereux Spratt (see Spratt 1886). See Blome 1678: 7. See also Friedman 1983: 77–90.

272 Coxere was a slave from 1657–1658. See Meyerstein 1945: 54–67.

273 Coxere suffered a number of imprisonments in England for his Quaker faith but that in Yarmouth lasted from late 1663 until April 1664 (Meyterstein 1945: 107). His is the only Barbary captivity narrative produced by a Quaker (albeit one who became a Quaker *after* his captivity) and his account was not published until the twentieth century. Accounts by Quakers of captivity at the hands of Native Americans were extremely popular and published on both sides of the Atlantic. See Dickinson 1699 and Bownas 1728.

274 Meyerstein 1945: 101.

9. Quaker Apocalypticism

The causal relationship between the positive estimation of Muslim religious tolerance in Quaker literature and the actual experience of Quakers appears simple enough to discern. However, we should not overlook the role of core Quaker religious convictions in this judgment and, in particular, the apocalypticism that created and shaped their discourse.[275] In many ways the 'Turks' were doing no more than demonstrating in their actions the veracity of the fundamental apocalyptic belief central to early Quaker faith. Early Friends were predisposed to potentially positive assessments of Muslim morality as their eschatology removed any particular preferential place for Christians, moving the locus of faith from a response to propositional knowledge of the Christian gospel to response to an experiential dispensation that they believed was available to all people. For example, as Fox wrote to Quakers in Algiers in 1683, using language that evoked both the expectation of the dispensation of God's spirit upon all people, found in the book of Joel, and belief in the arrival of the new covenant in which all will be able to know and be taught by God directly, found in the book of Jeremiah:[276]

> God, who made all, pours out of his spirit upon all men and women in the world, in the days of his new covenant, yea, upon whites and blacks, Moors, and Turks, and Indians, Christians, Jews, and Gentiles, that all with the spirit of God, might know God and the things of God, and serve and worship him in his spirit and truth, that he hath given them ... Now this is the Day of God's Gathering and therefore all must come to the Light, Grace, Truth, Power and Spirit of God in their own particulars.[277]

---

275 For the centrality of apocalypticism in understanding early Quakerism see, for example, Bruyneel (2010); Ingle (1992); Gwyn (1986). This 'apocalyptic turn' in conceptualising early Quakerism is a relatively recent phenomenon in Quaker historiography. See Ingle 1987.

276 Joel 2:28–32 (cf. Acts of the Apostles 2:17–21); Jeremiah 31:31–34.

277 Fox 1698: 492 (Ep. 388).

This thinking had already resulted in a number of encounters between Muslims and Quakers before the enslavement of Quakers in Barbary as Quakers sought to present their apocalyptic, universal 'Everlasting Gospel'[278] throughout the world. From their initial origins in the north of England in the late 1640s, itinerant Friends had spread their message in Ireland and Scotland by 1654, France, the American colonies and the West Indies by 1655, and by 1658 Quakers were proclaiming their gospel throughout mainland Europe, much of the Mediterranean, Surinam in South America, and even as far afield as the 'East Indies' (a vast area that ranged from Madagascar to Southeast Asia). This explosion of activity was 'one unmatched in the history of Christianity both in scope and speed'.[279] It is therefore unsurprising that early Friends had also sought to travel to Ottoman lands. Indeed, the Ottoman empire was somewhere that particularly drew them and which was clearly of considerable importance to them. In 1658 the fledgling, persecuted movement held a national collection to support those called to travel overseas and raised the considerable sum of £443 3s 5d of which £177 4s 19d, forty percent of the total raised, was expended on one mission expressly aimed at 'Turkey'.[280] The prophetic zeal that drove these Friends is apparent in the words of the most prominent Quaker who was part of this particular mission, John Perrot:

---

278 Revelation 14:6 'Then I sawe another Angel flie in the mids of heaven, having an everlasting Gospel, to preach unto them that dwell on the earth, and to every nation, and kindred, and tongue, and people' (Geneva Bible). For the use of this expression to describe the Quaker message see, for example, the title pages of Burrough 1660; Dewsbury 1689; Howgill 1655; Hubberthorn 1654. For the early Quakers it expressed both the apocalyptic character of the message that they delivered, and its eternal continuity with what they saw as the original worship set up by God. However, the expression 'Everlasting Gospel' was not unique to Quakers in this period. It was particularly associated with radical dissent and those who rejected reform of the church and proclaimed a restorationist message of some kind. See Hill 1984: 303 and Morton 1966.

279 Carroll 2010: 15.

280 For the accounts see London Yearly Meeting 1858: viii–ix. Friends actually spent a total of £490 13s 6d. Braithwaite provides a useful overview of this mission (1955: 420–426), but it has been superseded by Villani 1996: 33–45.

The word of the Lord came unto me ... saying write: My words in thy mouth I have putt to beare witness of my Everlasting Name, and behold I the Lord who have chosen thee from amongst men, doe Send thee into a farr country having given thee a sharpe Instrum[en]tt to thresh upon the Mountaines of Turkey.[281]

Although it could be said of these expeditions that 'there was never a more complete scorn of consequence and circumstance',[282] with little chance of much success – though as Sylvia Brown says, for a group with such an apocalyptic orientation, 'success', in terms of gaining converts, 'was not the point'[283] – famously this mission did result in one of its members, Mary Fisher, a servant from Yorkshire, gaining an audience before Sultan Mehmet IV at Adrianople in 1658.[284] Although she and two of her companions were sent home from Constantinople soon afterwards by an exasperated English ambassador, Sir Thomas Bendish, fed up at their disturbing behaviour that he believed was likely to bring the English as a whole into disrepute,[285] she was content that she had discharged her prophetic duty.[286] She later wrote:

---

281 Carroll 1971: 9 (Swarthmore MS 5/10, Friends House, London).

282 Braithwaite 1955: 410.

283 Brown 2007: 49.

284 Fisher was *not* one of the Quakers imprisoned in Malta (contra Matar 2001: 21). Only Katherine Evans and Sarah Cheevers were imprisoned in Malta (Baker 1663). See Cadbury 1974; Villani 2003.

285 Thurloe 1742: 287. A reaction that was quite common amongst English officials elsewhere in the lands controlled by the Sublime Porte. For example, in 1661 John Stubbs and Henry Fell were expelled from Egypt by the English consul Richard Bendish, having made it to Alexandria and possibly Cairo (see Baker 1662: 28; see also Baker's reference to the expulsion in 1663: 98). In the same year Daniel Baker and Richard Scosthrop were expelled from Smyrna (modern day Izmir) at the behest of the English ambassador Lord Winchilsea who issued a warrant against the troublesome Quakers proceeding any further. The warrant is reproduced in Baker's account of the events and gives us some insight into the perception of early Friends by English officials in the Ottoman empire and fears concerning the repercussions of their activities upon English trading interests (see Baker 1662: 11; also reproduced in Baker 1663: 95). Two unnamed Quaker women were similarly ejected from Scanderoon (Alexandretta), the port of Aleppo, by the English consul there (Croese 1696: 274) and another Quaker, simply named 'John', was beaten and expelled from Constantinople in 1661 by the ambassador (North 1744: 115).

286 The notion that a Quaker should return at once after discharging the message given to them was a feature of such 'missions'. As Robinson, who travelled to the Levant

I have borne my testimony to the king unto whom I was sent, and he was very noble unto me … He received the words of truth without contradiction, they do dread the word of God many of them … they are nearer the Truth than many nations, there is a love begot in me towards them that is endless.[287]

The story of Fisher's appearance before Mehmet IV is a fascinating one[288] that has had a considerable afterlife.[289] Whatever may have taken place, the account that emerged[290] is a largely positive one, in which the young Sultan[291] listened to her message respectfully, and offered her a military escort so that she did not come any harm as she continued on her way to Constantinople (an offer she declined).[292] The only moment of tension appears to have come when Fisher was asked her opinion on Muhammad, a subject on which she appears to have been reluctant to speak,[293] claim-

---

in 1657 wrote, on delivering his message: 'Thus my dear Friends, I cleared my Conscience, whether they would hear or forebear; wherein I found great peace with the Lord' (Baker 1663: 292). This way of understanding Quaker prophesying was something emphasised in the movement. See, for example, Fox's words in 1657 found in Barbour and Roberts 2004: 489–491. Mack may be right that this was particularly emphasised after the downfall of Nayler (1992: 213).

287 Mack 1992: 170. See also Brown 2007.

288 Karin Ådahl's study of the records of the Swedish embassy to Sultan Mehmed IV in 1657–1658 provide us with a remarkable insight into the context in which the encounter took place (see Ådahl 2006) although there is no mention of this incident, which though clearly of importance to Quakers, was of little significance to anyone else.

289 See Marr 2006: 3.

290 Quaker accounts of the event can be found in Bishop 1661: 19–20; Sewel 1722: 257–258; Besse 1753: 2.394 (though Sewel inaccurately dates this event to 1660; see Braithwaite 1955: 423). A non-Quaker account, which is somewhat sceptical about events and does not share Fisher's own interpretation, can be found in Croese (1696: 274–276). Croese maintains that he was unable to discover what exactly Fisher said in the interview (1696: 276) but assumes a rather narrow understanding of her mission. He wrote that Fisher must have informed the Sultan of 'the Errors of his Religion, and the Truth of hers' (1696: 275).

291 Mehmet IV was born in 1642 and so would have been about sixteen at the time of the meeting. He would go on to display an active interest in religion, notably encouraging the conversion of his non-Muslim subject peoples and the reforming of Islamic practice in the empire (Baer 2008). He would be rather less happy with the Jewish messianism of Shabbatai Zvi who converted to Islam in 1666 under intense pressure from Mehmed. See Goldish 2004; Scholem 1976.

292 Bishop 1661:19–20 (contra Matar 1998: 133).

293 The tension is evident in the earliest account found in Bishop (1661: 20) but all the more noticeable in Sewel's account, which in other respects is largely identical to

ing, perhaps somewhat disingenuously, that she did know him[294] but that if his words had come to pass, then he should be judged a true prophet[295] – a criterion for judging true and false prophets found in the book of Deuteronomy[296] and one familiar to early Friends, who had to defend their own claim to a movement of true prophets in the face of their critics.[297]

The response of the Sultan was in stark contrast to Fisher's earlier experience in Cambridge, England in 1653, where she was whipped through the streets of the city for preaching much the same message,[298] and in Boston, Massachusetts, in 1656, where she received similarly rough treatment at the hands of Puritan officials who detained her on her arrival, stripped her to check for the marks of witchcraft, jailed her for six weeks, burnt the Quaker books she had brought with her, and then forcibly ex-

---

that of Bishop, in which he adds the detail that Fisher answered the Sultan 'warily' (Sewel 1722: 258).

294 By the time of the meeting Fisher and her colleagues had been in Ottoman lands for some months and Fisher would also have had some knowledge of Muhammad, however imperfect, before undertaking the mission.

295 Bishop 1661: 20.

296 Deuteronomy 18:22. Brown seems unaware of the biblical origins of these criteria in her otherwise excellent treatment of Fisher (2007: 57).

297 They are referred to in numerous Quaker documents. For example, William Penn made use of them in refuting those who argued that Fox was a false prophet (incidentally maintaining that Muhammad did belong in this category; see Penn 1672: 50). Friends also had to use them to distinguish between true and false prophecy amongst their own members, something apparent, for example, in the case of James Milner who predicted that the world would end on November 15th 1653 (see Carroll 1985). The accusation that Quakers were false prophets was a common one; it comprises a significant part of Charles Leslie's exhaustive attack on Quakerism (1696). Fisher herself was hardly unfamiliar with such matters; she had co-authored a work entitled *False prophets and false teachers described* in 1652 from prison in York (although it is mostly an anti-clerical tract; Aldam et al. 1652).

However, it is interesting that according to the account we have Fisher did not raise the other possible criteria for determining the authenticity of a prophet found in the Old Testament and regularly discussed in polemical literature of the day, namely the criteria in Deuteronomy 13:2; Jeremiah 23:10–17, and Ezekiel 12:21–14:11. In the case of the latter two this is particularly striking as they include the idea that a prophet cannot be a true prophet if they are themselves immoral or encourage immorality amongst others. The morality of Muhammad and his message was regularly attacked in early modern England (see, for example, chapter four of Smith 1593, a text reprinted 17 times from 1593 to 1676 and a good indication of popular views on the matter; see also Birchwood 2013), as it had been since the earliest Christian anti-Muslim polemics (see, for example, John of Damascus, *De haeresibus* 101 [c. 730]).

298 Anon. 1654.

pelled her from the colony.[299] Indeed, Bishop appears to have been especially conscious of this contrast as his account of Fisher's favourable treatment appears in a text that was written in response to the recent execution of four Quakers in Boston by the Puritan authorities who had functionally made profession of Quakerism a capital offence, including, perhaps most famously, Mary Dyer who was hung in 1660 having been repeatedly banished but nonetheless returned to the colony to 'look their bloody laws in the face'.[300]

Similar apocalyptic motivations lay behind other Quaker journeys in Ottoman lands, such as those undertaken by George Robinson (1657),[301]

---

299 Bishop 1661: 5–13. Indeed, the Sultan's behaviour is all the more striking when contrasted with the prevailing view of the women of the Ottoman empire evident in English writing of the period. As Loomba states 'non-European women are depicted as either dangerous (sometimes grotesque, sometimes very beautiful), and needing to be purged and annihilated, or alienated from their own society' (2002: 28). Although see Holmber 2007 for a critique of this common generalisation.

300 See Bishop 1661; Burrough 1661. Although the expression is now proverbially associated with Dyer it is not one that Dyer herself used and was actually employed by Bishop to describe the activity of a number of Quakers in Boston who were undaunted by these laws (1661: 99).

301 Robinson's own account of his travels can be found in an appendix in Baker 1663: 277–292 (see also Sewel 1722:1.292–297; Besse 1753: 2.392–394, Fox 1658: 17–18; Cadbury 1972: 20). However, in addition to the Quaker's perspective on his mission, Stefano Villiani has made available the text of a fascinating record of Robinson's time in the Levant by an anonymous friar who encountered the young English cobbler turned prophet (see Villani 2001: 51–62). This reveals that the Quaker was the victim of a fraud and his encounter with 'a Turk in authority' (1663: 292) was nothing of the sort; the man he spoke to was a servant who had been dressed up by Catholics to convince Robinson that he had discharged his mission, and could now go home (Villani 2001: 57). Robinson's account of Quaker-Muslim encounter is invaluable but not quite in the way that the Quaker imagined.

Muslims are largely positively presented in Robinson's text, as hospitable and protective figures (1663: 281, 287), enquiring respectfully about his faith (1663: 289, 290). However, such an image is not universal and there are times when the presentation of the Turks and their religion is a rather equivocal one (contra Matar 1998a: 132). Robinson is threatened with violence and robbed by Turks (1663: 279, 286), and in Ramlah he is taken into a mosque and an attempt is made to force him to convert to Islam, where he is rescued from martyrdom by the intervention of an elderly 'tender' Turk who disagreed with the behaviour of his co-religionists (1663: 286–288; the incident was subsequently put down to the malicious plotting of the friars; see Cadbury 1972: 20). Robinson's refusal to give up his faith when threatened with death appears in the narrative as the reason for the respect that he gains from *all* religions: Turks, Greeks and Armenians (Baker 1663: 289; see Villani 2001: 59).

John Stubbs, Henry Fell, Daniel Baker and Richard Scosthrop (1661),[302] Katharine Evans and Sarah Cheevers (1658–1662),[303] John 'the Quaker' (1661),[304] John Philley and William Moore (1662)[305] – although in the case of the major expedition of 1661, the aim was to go even further afield, the Quakers taking papers addressed to the Emperor of China and the fabled Prester John.[306]

These journeys were predicated on the assumption that, as George Robinson, the teenage cobbler who made a journey, alone, to the Holy Land,[307] asserted, the Turks as much any other people could be gathered

---

302 Baker 1662, which includes copies of texts written during this mission, is a good indication of the apocalyptic motivations of those undertaking it. For example, 'The mighty, terrible, and glorious, and dreadful day of the eternal God is come and at hand' (1662: 13).

303 Baker 1663 contains letters from Evans and Cheevers that are indicative of this perspective.

304 Our sole source for the mission of this particular Quaker, who appeared in Constantinople in 1661 seeking an audience with the Sultan, comes from a report of Sir Dudley North, who had been a merchant in the Ottoman empire from 1661–1680; the motivations appear to have been apocalyptic but of a somewhat different kind. According to North the ambassador discovered that 'John' had a 'a Letter to the Grand Signor, very long, and canting; but the Substance was, to let him know, that he was the Scourge in God's Hand, with which he chastised the wicked Christians; and now their Wickedness was so great, that God by the Spirit had sent him, to let him know, that he must come forthwith to scourge them.' See North 1744: 115. See also Bent 1890: 658, 1893: xxv. See Grassby 1994. 'John the Quaker' was not John Perrot, who never mentioned reaching Constantinople and did not travel there after his release from prison in Rome. See Villani 1998: 179–181, Carroll 1971: 48, contra Matar 1998a: 133–134.

305 See Braithwaite 1955: 216. John Philley and William Moore tried to reach Ottoman territory through Hungary but their expedition met with abject failure as they fell into the hands of the Inquisition and found themselves accused of practising Turkish ways and seeking to flee to Ottoman territory to convert to Islam – something that religious radicals did, from time to time, the most notable being Adam Neuser, a leading Calvinist and then biblical Unitarian from Germany, who eventually 'turned Turk' (see Williams 1992: 1235). During their imprisonment and torture Philley and Mooore found themselves alongside captured Turks (our evidence for this comes from Besse 1753: 2.420–432; Besse claims that his account is a reproduction of a letter by Moore to William Caton in 1663). That the mission of Philley and Moore was expressly aimed at declaring the Quaker message to the Sultan is evident from an epistle of Fox from late 1662 (Cadbury 1972: 143).

306 Fox: 1831 II: 1. For Fox's letter the Emperor of China see Fox 1831: IV: 252–254. Elsewhere Fox confirmed that the main aim of the mission was to reach Prester John's country (Cadbury 1972: 187). See Meggitt 2011.

307 Robinson was actually hostile to the notion that he was visiting anywhere 'holy' (Baker 1663: 284; Villani 2001: 53); indeed, his journey could be seen, in part, as a

to God 'in this the Day of his gathering' and 'be blessed by him'[308] because they too, in the words of Daniel Baker, could respond to 'the eternal Light of our Lord Jesus which is the witness of God in every conscience, yea and to answer the same (in all men), which is to guide Nations, the Sons and Daughters of men into all truth'.[309] This final notion, was an avowedly Christocentric idea for the earliest Quakers, and expressed by them through the use of certain key New Testament texts, notably that of John 1:9: that Christ 'was the true light, which lighteth every man that cometh into the world' – a text that was taken to assume the universal presence of this Light in all people.

Such thinking may well also have lain behind two striking writings of John Perrot which directly address Muslims, *A visitation of love and gentle greeting of the Turk and tender tryal of his thoughts for God* (1656)[310] and *Blessed openings of a day of good things to the Turks written to the heads, rulers, ancients, and elders of their land, and whomsoever else it may concern* (1661), which give us a potential insight into the kind of message proclaimed by these Quaker 'missionaries'. These texts are remarkably eirenic works, which are unusual, in comparison with non-Quaker Christian writings of the time, not least because they do not attack the theology of Islam directly nor its prophet nor do they advocate baptism or any other sacrament.[311] Indeed, they make little use of the Bible, and in the case of the second tract, lack any direct quotations from it at all.[312] However, they

---

work of anti-pilgrimage. His reaction is similar to other English-speaking Protestant visitors to the region at the time, who viewed much of what they saw with indifference, scepticism or repugnance (see Lithgow 1614: Ov-P; Moryson 1617: 217–237; T. B. 1672; Biddulph 1609: 115–139). It is interesting that a Moroccan Muslim visitor to the Christian-controlled sites in Jerusalem, Salim Abdallah Ayyashi in 1663, did not display hostility towards them but felt it more appropriate to see such things from afar than to enter places of Christian worship. See Matar 2000: 42.

308 Robinson in Baker 1663: 292

309 Baker 1662: 13

310 Matar dates this tract to 1660 (1998a: 133). However, others have dated it earlier. See Carroll 1971: 34 who dates it to 1658. A copy of this tract in the Cambridge University Library has 1656 as its publication date. The date is important as if it is published before 1658 then it would be evidence of Perrot holding such views *before* he had travelled in Muslim-majority lands.

311 A point made by Matar 1998a: 134. For early Quakers all outward forms of religion were abolished in the light of the immediate presence of the indwelling, apocalyptic Christ. See Fox 1676, 1685.

312 Matar 1998a: 133.

are still avowedly Christian: Perrot's works are predicated upon Quaker understanding of the universality and total sufficiency of the immediate revelation of Christ in all humans. As Perrot says in *A Visitation:*

> God, who has been a stranger unto the inhabitants of the earth, is light ... hath sent his only begotten Son a Light into the world, whose light shineth in the consciences of every man that cometh into the World.[313]

The 'Everlasting Gospel' proclaimed by early Friends was an unusual one with striking consequences. As Pailin has noted in his influential survey of attitudes to other religions in seventeenth and eighteenth century Britain, the Quaker message was distinctive because it 'challenges rather than supports' aspects of the traditional self-understanding of Christianity'.[314]

It is perhaps all the more surprising because one might assume such a totalising, universal eschatological vision, however potentially benevolent in its attitude towards Muslims, would still deny the particularity of their religion; it might be assumed to take the form of 'millenarian imperialism'

---

313 Perrot 1656: 11–12. It is therefore not fully accurate for Matar to say that Perrot does not rely for 'legitimacy on the inerrancy of the Christian revelation' (1998a: 134). It may not be an *orthodox* understanding of Christian revelation but it is certainly one that the early Friends regarded as inerrant. Both documents are also predicated on the existence of a peculiarly Christian soteriological predicament that would be alien to a Muslim reader – that, without redemption, all human beings suffer the consequences of the Fall. Whilst the disobedience of Adam and Eve is mentioned in the Qur'an (Q 20: 120), and hadith, such an idea is not derived from these sources.

314 Pailin 1984: 134. The Quaker travels to the east had one unexpected and enduring legacy. In 1673 a gruesome eyewitness account appeared of the torture and execution of three Quakers who arrived in Constantinople and, in typical Quaker fashion, disrupted worship, albeit in a mosque (Wilson 1673). The text was republished a number of times (Elias 1674, 1681) with minor but significant alterations that indicate that it is a work of fiction (see Villani 1996: 157–159 and 1998; contra Matar 1998a: 136; Braithwaite 1979: 668). The events are described as having occurred in three different years – 1672, 1673 and 1680 and in the first account the four eminent Quakers who began the journey are described as coming from Yorkshire, in the second their county of origin is given as Gloucestershire, and in the 1681 edition, no provenance is given. Nowhere in Quaker records of the time, nor those of the English officials and merchants in Constantinople, do we find reference to this sensational incident or the names of those who allegedly undertook the journey. This story tells us more about anti-Quaker and anti-Ottoman prejudice in England in the late seventeenth century, and the persistent interest in the exotic and macabre amongst the pamphlet buying public, than anything else.

of the kind identified by Hill.[315] However, this does not seem to have been the case, as we can see from the striking text that Fox wrote in 1680 in response to reports of abuse of Quaker slaves in Algiers. His epistle *To The Great Turk And King At Argiers [sic] : Together With A Postscript Of George Pattison's Taking The Turks, And Setting Them On Their Own Shore.*[316]

In this work Fox makes his case by holding the recipients accountable to the demands of their own revealed text and does so by quoting carefully and extensively from the Qur'an, giving both the sura number and the page number in Ross' translation of 1649. Over thirty different direct quotations taken from widely different sections of the Qur'an are employed to make the author's case. So, for example, he protests against the injustice in the treatment of the slaves by noting that:

'He that slayeth an innocent person shall be punished as if he had slain the whole world; and he that shall give his life, shall be recompensed as if he had given life to the whole world. Now, hath not your practice herein been contrary to your Alcoran, as in chap. v. p. 64, 65.[317]

---

315 Hill 1990: 232. See Ingle 1992.
316 Fox 1680 (also found in Fox 1706: 77–87; Fox 1831 VI: 77–92). Fox made a similar argument, revisiting some of his Qur'anic quotations, in a text of 1688 entitled *An answer to the speech or decalration [sic] of the great Turk, Sulton [sic] Mahomet.* This text was a response by Fox to an alleged letter from Mehmet IV to the Emperor Leopold issued before the campaign that would lead to the defeat of the Ottoman forces and their Hungarian Protestant allies before the gates of Vienna in 1683. Fox reprinted the Sultan's words in 1688 in a tract that also contained a letter Fox claimed to have written in 1683 which condemned Mehmet IV's hubris and, amongst other things, used the Qur'an to argue that the Sultan had fallen short of the moral standards expected of a Muslim and would suffer the consequences (Mehmet had been toppled from power in 1687, thus confirming Fox in his judgement on the matter).
    Although roughly similar in length to his letter of 1680, Fox deploys only six quotations from the Qur'an and all these quotations are quite brief. Fox is less precise in his handling of the text, only occasionally giving the number of the sura or page number relating to Ross' translation. The references to the Qur'an in the overall rhetorical structure of the work are not as central as they had been in the earlier epistle. In this letter we do not find a Fox as intent on persuading his audience as he was in 1680, so much as someone intent on reprimanding the recipient, albeit by once again recalling the Muslim reader to the moral standards of their religion (albeit a Quaker, Christological interpretation of it).
317 Fox 1680: 5 (Fox 1831 VI: 80).

And again, Mahomet saith, chap. cv. p. 391, 'He that devours the substance of orphans, and the bread of the poor, blasphemes against the law of God, and misery is upon him.[318]

In addition to such quotations, Fox also displays a grasp of the major themes of the Qur'an, such as the justice of God and the impending judgement of humans, themes to which he repeatedly returns. He at no point questions the authority of the text itself, the religion it espouses, or its prophet. This despite being dependent upon Ross' prejudiced text, and reading the Qur'an from within a culture that popularly judged it to be the work of a diabolical fraud and an incoherent jumble,[319] something which Ross' poor translation did nothing to rectify.

Instead the Qur'an is used to demonstrate that the behaviour of the Turks, in their treatment of the Quaker slaves, fell below the moral standards that their scripture demanded of them. How they behaved is, in Fox's judgement, against the 'law of the great god, and your Alcoran' – an argument that assumes a fundamental commonality between the two, an unusual admission for an early modern Christian; in fact, according to MacLean and Matar, almost without exception.[320] In Fox's argument he is careful to disassociate the immorality of Muslims from the morality of the religion, whilst contemporaries were quick to argue that the immorality of the latter actually caused the former.[321] Indeed, he does not even assume that the immorality he was attacking was endemic amongst Muslims, a common prejudice of the time.[322] Fox had already argued that knowledge of God and righteous actions could be greater amongst

---

318 Fox 1680: 10 (Fox 1831 VI: 84).
319 Indeed Quakers even found their own mode of discourse in print and speech likened to the Qur'an in this respect: 'And whereas thou sayest, The Quakers words are jumbled together, so that every Line hath no sence in it: and thou resemblest them to the Turks Alkaron' (Fox 1667a: 7).
320 Fox 1680: 3 (Fox 1831 VI: 78). See MacLean and Matar 2011: 37.
321 See, for example, Hanmer 1586.
322 Matar 1999: 109–127.

those who did not know the Christian scriptures than amongst those that did,[323] and in this text he demonstrates just such a conviction.

Fox even appears to show some awareness of the possible sensitivities of his Muslim readers in the arguments that he makes by employing terminology that reflects Islamic preferences, even if it would also be acceptable to him. So, for example, he refers to God regularly in this epistle at the 'great god', an expression that equates to Qur'anic terminology as rendered by Ross, and is an expression otherwise not found in Fox's writings. He calls some biblical figures 'prophets' who are labelled such in the Qur'an but are not referred to in this way in the Christian Bible (for example, Joseph and David). Fox's Christology in this document is also, at times, decidedly Qur'anic: he emphasises the prophetic identity of Jesus and his role in judgement day, preferring to refer to him as the 'son of Mary' or a similar expression, rather than the more obviously contentious title 'son of God'.[324] His reading is not without its problems: it is fundamentally Christocentric and he seems unaware that, for a Muslim audience, it would not follow that whatever Jesus commands in the New Testament would be regarded as binding because of his prophetic status in the Qur'an, and so his repeated claim that Jesus' command to love one's enemies is incumbent upon Muslims too, fails to have any purchase.[325] He also regularly employed the formula 'Mahomet saith' which would be problematic for a Muslim reader as it appears to imply Muhammad's authorship of the Qur'an.

Nonetheless, although Matar is possibly somewhat anachronistic in his use of the term 'dialogue' here, and does not recognise the essentially Quaker Christian reading of the Qur'an by Fox, he asserts, with good reason, that Fox 'was breaking new ground in Christian-Muslim dialogue by positioning himself in the Muslim camp'.[326] It is, perhaps, all the more impressive as Fox had clearly moved beyond his earlier knowledge of Islam which included the common belief that 'Mahomet' was an idol wor-

---

323 A point that was vital in Quaker arguments for the supremacy of direct revelation against those who held that revelation should be limited to Christian scripture. See, for example, Fox 1671 (Fox 1831 IV: 387–406). See also Thomas 1996: 65.

324 For example, Fox 1680: 1, 4, 10 (Fox 1831 VI: 77, 79, 84); Parrinder 2003: 22.

325 Fox 1680: 10–11 (Fox 1831 VI: 84).

326 Matar 1989: 272.

shipped by Muslims[327] – perhaps under the influence of Quakers with direct knowledge of Muslims and a favourable opinion of the morality and faithfulness of most of them, such as Stephen Smith, whom Fox seems to have known well.[328] Certainly *To the Great Turk And King At Argiers* (1680) marks a change from the first text that Fox addressed directly to a Muslim which he had written some twenty years earlier,[329] and which does not display much knowledge of Islam, shows no evidence that Fox had, at that stage, read the Qur'an nor that he was either willing or able to articulate his message any differently for a Muslim audience.[330] It only makes three references to Muhammad and these are negative.[331]

---

327 See Fox 1659: 3. The notion that Muslims worshipped a statue of Muhammad had first become prominent in the eleventh century in northern Europe (see Tolan 2002; Cesare 2012). Fox's position changed completely on this subject as a result of the enslavement of Quakers and his reading of the Qur'an. By 1687 Muslims were, for Fox, enemies of idolatry and favoured by God for this reason (1694: 587; 1831 II: 328).

328 See, for example, Penney 1911: 264. See also Smith 1676. Smith was keen to distinguish the high standards of morality shown by most 'Turks', in his experience, with that displayed by various Barbary corsairs and some other 'high-minded' Muslims (Smith 1676: 7). Fox's interest in Islam should not be pushed too far though: other than in Fox's *Answer to the Great Turk* (1688), mentioned above, he makes no further use of the Qur'an, neither quoting or alluding to it, in his extensive writings, and only refers to it in passing elsewhere. His interest in the Qur'an, exceptional though it was, appears to have been entirely pragmatic.

329 *To the Turk and all under his authority* (1660a). The text of this letter can also be found in Fox 1831: IV: 216–221. The epistle is similar to others addressed to world leaders and written in the same period (see, for example, *For The Emperor of China* [Fox 1831: IV: 252–254] and were sent with the expedition of John Stubbs, Henry Fell, Richard Scosthrop and Daniel Baker in 1661. Matar is right to draw attention to *An Epistle to all Professors in the Christian World, also to the Jews and the Turks* (1673; Fox 1831: 407–414); another text is addressed (in part) to Muslims but this is not the earliest text Fox addressed to them (contra Matar 1989: 271). Indeed, Fox appears to have written a number of other texts to Muslims that we do not possess, including a batch of epistles in 1661 (*To the great Cham of Tartary, To the great Moghul,* and *To the King of Suratt;* see Cadbury 1939: 77) as well as an address to the *Empereur of Marocco's Embassador* (1681; Cadbury 1939: 171) – which he appears to have delivered in person when Muhammad bin Hadu was visiting England in 1681–1682 (Cadbury 1939: 171, 1952: 737).

330 The 1660 work does include the Turks within those who have access to the light that has enlightened all that come into the world, and they are treated as potential members of the people of God, which in itself, according to Matar, is a significant difference from Fox's contemporaries (1989: 271). Such a conviction is a recurring theme in Fox and something that the Quaker James Nayler had argued publicly as early as 1653 (see Fox and Nayler 1653: 21).

331 In one reference, Muhammad is described as having deceived the Turks (Fox 1660a: 8), and in the other two it appears that Fox believed that Muslims worshipped Mu-

Fox's addition to *The Great Turk And King At Argiers* of the *Postscript Of George Pattison's Taking The Turks, And Setting Them On Their Own Shore*[332] is also an important part of Fox's argument as well as an indication of the views of Islam held by other Quakers. The narrative is a compelling one and gives an account of the famous case of George Pattison and Thomas Lurting, who, when captured by Barbary privateers, non-violently turned the tables on their captors, and gained their freedom without harming either the 'Turks' or their Quaker consciences. Running the risk of falling into the hands of other privateers and the Spanish, they then sailed to North Africa and returned the 'Turks' to their homeland, refusing demands, along the way, that they sell their prisoners into slavery.[333] Only then did they finally return to England.

There are many interesting questions raised by this narrative. It is, for example, an inversion of a common trope in Barbary captivity accounts, where slaves rise up and slaughter those that have enslaved them, perhaps most famously seen in the bloody account of John Rawlins;[334] a narrative in which the providence of God and the moral obligations of humans are diametrically opposed to the understanding within the *Postscript*.'[335] For Rawlins, God's providence is evident in the successful slaughter of the Turks and renegades, for which he and the other slaves give thanks, whereas Lurting is reassured, from the outset of his account that he will be delivered by God, but that this deliverance must be by means of non-

---

hammad in some way (1660a: 10, 11). For another example of Fox believing that Muslims worshipped Muhammad see Fox 1661b: 15; 1831 IV: 279.

332 The original event seems to have taken place in 1663, but was first written down by Lurting in 1680. See also Lurting 1710.

333 Fox 1680: 18 (Fox 1831 VI: 90).

334 See Rawlins 1622. See also Anon. 1622 for a similar incident and the Phippen Memorial, St Mary's, Truro (now Truro cathedral) which recounts how Owen Phippen in 1627, after seven years of slavery, led a successful, bloody mutiny against his slavers (I would like to thank Jo Esra for this reference). D'Aranda recounts a similar episode, albeit one which failed (1666: 201). The Icelanders captured by Murat Reis seem to have attempted to do the same (Lewis 1993: 244). See also Starr 1965: 41 fn. 11 for examples of revolts by captives *before* they reached Barbary. For a similar, successful revolt of Muslim slaves, see Pitts 1731: 89.

335 The reader is told to 'hearken then I pray you to this following relation, and learne hereby, as I said, both to give God the praise of all deliverances, and to instruct one another in the absolute duties of Christianity' (Rawlins 1622: 4). The victorious slaves gather, following the final battle, to sing a Psalm and 'give thanks to God for their deliverance' (1622: 28).

violence. Such is his commitment to this that he claims to have said to the non-Quaker sailors, as they discussed their plans for freedom, that 'if I knew any of them that offered to touch a Turk, I would tell the Turks myself'.[336] It is fitting that the version of Lurting's account published in 1710 begins with Isaiah 2:4 – 'They shall beat their Swords into Ploughshares, and their Spears into Pruning-hooks'. The underlying events are clearly quite exceptional, but it should also be noted that the Muslim subjects in the *Postscript*, although spared their lives at the behest of pacifist Quakers, are functionally denied 'authentic heterogeneity'[337] in the account and treated as an undifferentiated mass. In this case the Quakers may have demonstrated that they loved their enemies but such love did not extended to showing any particular interest in them (though communication does appear to have been something of a problem).

Fox's inclusion of the narrative could also be said, however, to be eschatologically determined. Quaker self-identity, from the outset of the movement, was focused upon a distinctive and self-conscious morality that was understood to distinguish them from other, 'apostate' Christians. For early Friends, their moral lives witnessed to the new apocalyptic, prelapsarian perfection that they claimed was now accessible to all.[338] While such an attention to morality had obvious problems, and Quakers were regularly criticised for falling short of the perfection that they preached, it also had the advantage of creating an arena in which a person, largely disempowered by the circumstances of slavery, could exhibit meaningful agency of some kind. Indeed, in the letters that Fox wrote to the captives in Algiers and Morocco, although essentially letters of consolation and exhortation, he emphasised the need for the slaves to realise that within

---

336 Fox 1680: 16 (Fox 1831 VI : 89).

337 Baker 2001: 11.

338 The most famous statement of this belief can be found in Fox 1694: 17–18 (Fox 1831 I: 84–85): 'Now was I come up in spirit, through the flaming sword, into the paradise of God. All things were new, and all the creation gave another smell unto me than before, beyond what words can utter. ... And the Lord showed me, that such as were faithful to him, in the power and light of Christ, should come up into that state in which Adam was before he fell.' There were, of course, variations and developments in what exactly Friends meant by the attainability of perfection in this life (see Moore 2000: 85–87; Damrosch 1996: 93–107), but it was a prominent characteristic of early Quaker faith, and one consistently attacked by its critics (Underwood 1997: 59–61).

their constrained circumstances, their manner of life and conversation could function to make both Muslims and others in Barbary conscious of the light of Christ within them.

> And my desire is, that the Lord may preserve you all, that do meet in the name of Jesus, that in your lives, and conversations, and words, you may preach righteousness, and holiness, and godliness, and the life of truth; so that you may answer the spirit of God, both in the Turks and Moors, and the rest of the captives; that God's city may be set upon the holy hill there, which cannot be hid; but that all may see it with the light wherewith Christ hath enlightened every man that cometh into the world ... And as you do walk in the light, grace, spirit, and gospel, you may turn others to it. That you may have unity with them in it; and that they may come out of the spiritual prison of death, darkness, and corruption, and captivity, into the liberty of the sons of God in Christ Jesus. Amen.[339]

Interestingly, we have here a reversal of the usual subjectivities we would expect in seventeenth century English constructions of the ethnic and religious 'other'. Rather than only being interested in their own 'gaze', the Quakers were encouraged to think of themselves as needing to be judged righteous in the eyes of the Turks.[340] It is important to note that such a concern was not justified with reference to its utility to the captives, such as the likelihood that it might lead to their freedom, but in terms of its value to the Muslim.

Quaker apocalypticism is, perhaps, all the more surprising given the uses to which apocalyptic was put in the writings of Britons in the early modern period.[341] Eschatology had long had a part to play in Christian anti-Islamic rhetoric, as a response to the perceived and real threat posed by Islamic empires,[342] but it became particularly significant during the Reformation when it was given a more overt scriptural warrant through

---

339 Fox 1698: 455 (Ep. 366 [1682]).
340 See also Fox 1674 (Fox 1831 V: 6).
341 See Matar 1998a: 153–183. See also MacGinn 1994, 1998; Setton 1992; Toon 1970.
342 See, for example, Lerner's study of the persistence of the Cedar of Lebanon Prophecy (Lerner 1983). Interestingly, prophecies by Turks themselves were also used in such a way, as can be seen in the popularity of Bartholomaeus Georgievicz's translation of the prophecy of the Red Apple (Setton 1992: 29–46).

the malleable nature of specifically apocalyptic texts of Daniel and Revelation.[343] As Matar notes, 'as Protestants in England, Scotland and on the continent watched Ottoman military advances, they started to treat eschatology as the final weapon in their hands';[344] and the eventual triumph of the kingdom of Christ, equated with Protestantism, was thereby assured.

Of course, it would be rash to claim that such thinking had the same level of currency in English culture throughout the seventeenth century; it is well known that there were moments of intense apocalyptic anxiety in that period,[345] as England went through the paroxysms of social and religious turmoil, fuelled by the disorientating experience of civil war, revolution and restoration, and the anticipation aroused by messianic expectations, such as those of the Fifth Monarchists[346] or the followers of Shabbatai Zvi;[347] claims about which both heightened and also discredited the authority of apocalyptic exegetes.[348]

It is also the case that Quaker apocalypticism could be said to be rather more variegated and also rather more conventional a phenomenon than I have portrayed here. A more literal, chronological reading of apocalyptic, similar to that of other early modern Protestants, may have been present in the opening decades of the movement. Such readings certainly did

---

343 'The Turk became associated with the Papal enemy of God – both of whom were identified with the "Little horn" in the Book of Daniel and the "Beast" in Revelation' (Matar 1998a: 153).

344 Matar 1998a: 154.

345 See, for example, Ball 1979; Gribben 2000.

346 Fifth Monarchists, who were a discernible movement from 1649, attempted to seize London in January 1661 in preparation for the arrival of 'King Jesus', who they believed would rule the fifth kingdom predicted in Daniel 2:24–45, the kingdom 'that shall never be destroyed'. For the Fifth Monarchists this referred to a literal millennial kingdom on earth (Revelation 20). See Capp 1972.

347 See Goldish 2004; Scholem 1976. Although Zvi was based in Turkey, his impact upon the wider Jewish diaspora was considerable. For example, in his entry for February 19th, 1666, the diarist Samuel Pepys refers to a Jewish follower in London taking bets on Zvi becoming 'King of the World' and proving himself the Messiah within the next couple of years (2003: 586).

348 Indeed, astrological rather than biblical millenarianism may well have been rather more robust in the face of regular disappointments, such as that of 1656 and 1660 (Capp 1979; Hill 1993: 301). However, this should not be exaggerated. Biblical apocalyptic speculation remained significant in the late seventeenth century too. See Johnston 2011; Koshin 1984.

have their place as tracts written by Margaret Fell to convert Jews in Amsterdam indicate,[349] although the notoriety achieved by James Nayler, who, in 1656, was tried for blasphemy for something that looked, to outsiders at least, to be a scandalous and presumptuous act in which he claimed to be Christ returned, may well have led to its eclipse.[350] However, these caveats aside, it is clear that a specifically Quaker apocalyticism had a distinctive role to play in the unusual estimation of Islam evidenced in this early modern English sect. The striking consequence of this particular configuration of apocalypticism should also provoke us to think again about the character of apocalypticism itself. Although there have been some recent attempts to rethink and revalue the role of apocalyptic in human imagination and, in particular, the foundational imagination of the 'West', and to view it as a catalyst for constructive as well as destructive transformations of society,[351] it is still often viewed as the preserve of the 'unstable',[352] and is rarely judged as anything other than antithetical towards inter-religious encounter.[353] For all its obvious limitations, and historical specificity, the early Quaker-Muslim experience appears to indicate otherwise.

---

349 Bruyneel 2010; Guibbory 2001.

350 See Bittle 1986; Damrosch 1996.

351 See, for example, Fried 2004; Hall 2009; Lisboa 2011; Lyons and Økland 2009; Popkin 2001; Westport 2008.

352 Cook 2005: 2.

353 See, for example, Gow 1995; Setton 1992. The exception to this is apocalyptically motivated Christian Zionism which can appear to be philosemitic (see Karp and Sutcliffe 2011) though in such thinking Jews can often be said to be 'not valued on their own terms but as part of the Christian story' (Wright 2009: 83), as the means towards a Christian messianic age.

10. Conclusion

As Timothy Marr notes in his work *The Cultural Roots of American Islamicism*, 'Westerners from as far back as the Crusades have imagined it [Islam] as a post-Christian provocation to which they have responded by devising an archive of ideological fictions aimed at defusing the heretical rivalry of what Edward Said has called its "original cultural effrontery"'.[354] However, even when enslaved (or perhaps, especially when enslaved?) it is fair to say that seventeenth century Quakers did not generally view Islam in such a manner. They rarely used language that implied such an estimation. If we were to push for a reason why this particular Christian 'Western' movement did not behave as Said and others might expect, I think the answer lies in the nature of early Quaker apocalyptic itself and the cultural form this took. In its own distinctive claims, embodied in the awkward social and linguistic practices, what Bauman called its 'rhetoric of impoliteness',[355] it positioned itself as the ultimate cultural effrontery, in which apostate Christendom, and Islam, and indeed all outward religions, were in the same category, with none privileged in the face of the Quaker's apocalyptic gospel nor any excluded. Indeed, the parallels between Islam and Quakerism in this respect were not lost on contemporaries in this period. No wonder we find that in seeking to dismiss the Muslim claims about the revelations given to Muhammad, an Anglican writer such as Charles Leslie at the end of the seventeenth century could assert that these were 'as groundless as the delusions of Fox'.[356]

The encounters I have examined, and the images they helped generate, are sufficiently striking and anomalous in the history of Christian-Muslim relations as to have provided ample justification for the subject of the study. Indeed, not only the encounters themselves but also the consequences of these encounters could provide reason enough for our undertaking – there is, for example, a clear link between the origins of

---

354 Marr 2006: 4.
355 Bauman 1983.
356 Pailin 1984: 87.

the movement to abolish the Atlantic slave trade in Africans and the Quaker experience of Barbary slavery, evident in the famous German-town Declaration of 1688, the first collective Christian statement against slavery.[357] The Quakers who composed this document were clearly influenced in their thinking by their knowledge of the enslavement of their co-religionists in Barbary. The text begins with a plea for empathy and reminds the reader of their fear of being captured at sea by 'Turks' and sold into slavery, a plea that was all the more compelling because it was a subject that touched the lives of the signatories. At the time they wrote the text, Friends were collecting funds for the redemption of Quaker slaves[358] known to the writers. Daniel Pastorius, one of those signing the text and who probably had a considerable part to play in its composition, had arrived on the *America* in 1683, a journey that nearly resulted in his own capture by a corsair.[359] The captain of the ship was the Quaker Joseph Wasey, a regular visitor to Pennsylvania,[360] who owned land in Philadelphia (which was only a few miles from Germantown).[361] Wasey was a slave in Salé when the Declaration was composed, having been enslaved in 1685.[362] Also languishing in Morocco in 1688 was George Palmer, the son of a leading Quaker in Philadelphia, for whom the

---

357 The full text of the Germantown Declaration can be found in Hughes 2007: 268–270. See also Carey 2010, 2012, and Gerbner 2007. Although often regarded as having little practical consequence, Carey has made a case for re-evaluating its significance (see Carey 2010, 2012).

358 It should be noted that this was something complicated by their unusual religious identity. Becoming Quaker whilst enslaved may have had its benefits, as Matar has observed (2001a: 30), not least the organised, ongoing support of other Friends, but it also caused problems. It seems to have closed some potential routes to freedom: Friends in Morocco were informed that they could not be redeemed in exchange for weapons, something that was a common practice at the time (Carroll 1985–1986: 71). It also complicated others: such was the dislike of Quakers that their inclusion in plans for general redemptions of English captives was by no means certain (MfS 1: 142–143 [1680]; see also Carroll 1985–1986: 72).

359 See Myers 1912: 392.

360 We know, for example, that he not only captained the *America* but also the *Grey-hound* for a voyage bringing colonists in 1677. Sheppard 1992: 84, 141.

361 Sheppard 1992: 84.

362 Wasey was captured by 1685 (MfS 4: 93), and, after a lengthy period in a dungeon (MfS 6.260), was redeemed by early 1691 (MfS 7: 54). During his time in Morocco Wasey managed to have an audience before the Emperor Moulay Ismail to plead the case of the Quakers, and gave an account of his 'innocent conversion and religion; which he heard with moderation; though he often kills men in cold blood at his

Monthly Meeting (the regional Quaker grouping of which Germantown Meeting was a member) was actively collecting funds in order to effect his redemption.[363] Palmer was amongst the final group of survivors who were redeemed in 1701 having been a slave for sixteen years. In addition to these direct links, there were no doubt other reasons why the signatories of the Germantown Declaration would be all too conscious of the reality of Barbary slavery; for example, the ship the *Kent*, which had been used to take 230 Quaker colonists to Pennsylvania in 1677, was captured the following year, leading to the predicament of Bartholomew Cole, the Muslim-turned-Quaker discussed above.[364]

The unusual, universal apocalyptic perspective of Friends may also have contributed to the unusual interest some showed in Ibn Tufayl's *Hayy Ibn Yaqzan* (The Self-Taught Philosopher), an eleventh century Arabic, Muslim allegory which was taken as confirming their belief that God could be known directly by anyone, irrespective of knowledge derived from others or the written revelations of revealed religion.[365]

---

pleasure' (Epistles from the Yearly Meeting of Friends Held in London 1: 57–58 [1691]).

    Wasey fared better than at least some of his crew. In a letter from 1693, from one of the captives, James Ellis (not a Quaker but the son of one), we are told that 'Wasey's Negro' was killed by his task master for 'only owning himself a Christian' (MfS 9: 22). The unnamed man may have originally been Wasey's slave, as some Quakers did own slaves in this period (though not in the British Isles, where slavery was considered illegal, even if the reality was somewhat more complex; see Hulsebosch 2006). However, the language used in the letter could indicate that the African was one of the regular crew on the ship. As Boltser notes, by the early seventeenth century 'a black seafaring tradition had taken root within the embryonic Anglo-American world' (1997: 9) which included both those who were free or freed (seafaring allowed a degree of autonomy and equality largely unparalleled in other contexts – though from a later period, the life of the Quaker Paul Cuffe provides an example of this; Wiggins 1996).

363 The minutes for Philadelphia Monthly Meeting of 1692 mention that £83 18s had been collected for this purpose (Minutes of Philadelphia Monthly Meeting 24th 4m 1692: 116). See also MfS 11: 219.

364 See Anon. 1682.

365 The text was first translated into English by the Quaker George Keith in 1674, and Robert Barclay made use of it in his *Apology* in a section concerned with demonstrating the veracity of belief in the inward Light (Barclay 1678: 126; see Elmarsafy 2009a). However, the importance of this text to Quakers should not be overestimated. Keith's interest was unusual, the translation and publication apparently undertaken at his own initiative, and whilst Barclay's use of a Muslim thinker in a work of Christian theology is unusual, as Matar has rightly observed (Matar 1998a: 100),

Given the rapid growth in innovative and challenging scholarship on cultural intersections between early modern England and the Ottoman empire and its environs that has taken place in the last decade or so, initiated by Matar,[366] but also evident in the writings of a range of other literary and cultural scholars,[367] a comprehensive study of the relations between early Quaker and Muslims is overdue.[368] It is clear that most early Quaker records of Quaker-Muslim encounter do not simply replicate the prevailing anti-Muslim prejudices and polarities evident in many of the discourses characteristic of subsequent centuries, and which reflect and constitute the ideologies of European imperial rule. Whilst this may well be, in part, a consequence of the early Quakers inhabiting a world *before* Orientalism, it is also undoubtedly a consequence of the fact that Quaker identity in the seventeenth century deliberately, self-consciously, problematized exactly those dominant or incipient national and religious identities that helped create orientalist ways of thinking about, and presenting, Muslims and Islam.[369]

Gerald MacLean has stated that: 'examining how and why Europeans represented the Ottoman Empire, and the Muslim world more generally ... is arguably the most exciting and important scholarly endeavour on the

---

Hayy Ibn Yaqzan is not particularly prominent when viewed within the context of the overall argument of the *Apology*. By 1800 and the ninth edition of the *Apology*, the passage had been excised. Even Keith, who was expelled from the Society in 1694 and converted to Anglicanism, would distance himself from such ideas, attacking Barclay's *Apology* and roundly deriding the doctrine that he had claimed was evident in, amongst other things, Ibn Tufayl's writing (Keith 1702).

366 See especially Matar's important trilogy: 1998, 1999, 2005.

367 Notably, Andrea 2007; Birchwood 2007; Birchwood and Dimmock 2005; MacLean 2004, 2007; MacLean and Matar 2011; Parker 1999.

368 Matar has laid an important foundation (1989, 1998a). The only other work of direct relevance, the contribution of Vlasblom (2011), is derivative of Matar and has a number of serious and significant lacunae.

369 This valuation of the non-Christian 'other' may also have played a part in the unusual suggestion by the Quakers William Penn (1693) and John Bellers (1710) that the peace of Europe could only be ensured if the Turks be included in a future European parliament – and given significant power within it (in Penn's plan, second only to Germany, equal to France and greater than Britain) – although both Quakers put forward largely pragmatic and secular arguments for this proposal. See Matar 1998a: 137.

agenda of early modern cultural studies today'.[370] It should also be of considerable significance for those interested in the study of inter-religious relations. Examining the distinctive records of early Quaker-Muslim encounter, far from being an exercise in the inconsequential, should play a necessary and valuable part in such a vital undertaking.

---

370 MacLean 2007: 9. Though we should bear in mind that the term 'European' is a problematic one to use in analysing the seventeenth century, as 'neither Christian nor Muslim imagined a "European" culture before the eighteenth century' (Goffman 1992: 4).

Bibliography

Seventeenth-century English spellings and punctuation have been retained. Dates in square brackets denote date of original composition or publication.

Primary Texts

Addison, Lancelot (1679) *The first state of Mahumedism, or, An account of the author and doctrines of that imposture by the author of The present state of the Jews.* London: W. Crooke.

Aldam, Thomas et al. (1652) *False prophets and false teachers described.* London: s.n.

Anon. (1597) *The policy of the Turkish empire. The first booke.* London: John Windet.

Anon. (1622) *A relation strange and true, of a ship of Bristol named the Iacob of 120. tunnes.* London: Nathaniel Butter.

Anon. (1653) *The Querers and Quakers cause at the second hearing.* London: Nathaniel Brooke.

Anon. (1654) *The first new persecution, or, A true narrative of the cruel usage of two Christians [Quakers].* London: Giles Calvert.

Anon. (1659) *Strange and terrible newes from Cambridge a true relation of the Quakers bewitching of Mary Philips out of the bed from her husband in the night, and transformed her into the shape of a bay mare.* London: C. Brooks.

Anon. (1676) *A true narrative of a wonderful accident which occur'd upon the execution of a Christian slave at Aleppo in Turky.* London: Dorman Newman.

Anon. (1680) *The case of many hundreds of poor English-captives in Algier together with some remedies to prevent their increase: humbly represented to both Houses of Parliament.* London: s.n.

Anon. (1682) *A list of ships taken since July, 1677 from his Majesties subjects, by the corsairs of Algier. With their names, masters names, and places to which they belong'd, and time of taking: with a modest estimate of the loss.* London: Richard Janeway.

Anon. (1712) *Four treatises concerning the doctrine, discipline and worship of the Mahometans.* London: B. Lintott.

Baker, Daniel (1662) *A clear voice of truth sounded forth, and as an ensign lifted up and displayed in answer to the proceedings of the Christians by name in Asia.* London: s.n.

Baker, Daniel (ed.) (1663) *A true account of the great tryals and cruel sufferings undergone by those two faithful servants of God, Katherine Evans and Sarah Cheevers ... to which is added a short relation from George Robinson.* Second edition. London: R. Wilson.

Barclay, Abram Rawlinson (1841) *Letters, &c., of Early Friends and Epistles of Counsel and Exhortation*. London: Harvey and Darton.

Barclay, Robert (1673) *A catechism and confession of faith.* s.i.: s.n.

Barclay, Robert (1676) *Roberti Barclaii Theologiae verè Christianae*. Amsterdam: Jacob Claus.

Barclay, Robert (1678) *An apology for the true Christian divinity, as the same is held forth and preached by the people called, in scorn, Quakers*. Aberdeen?: s.n.

Baxter, Richard (1696) *Reliquiae Baxterianae, or, Mr. Richard Baxters narrative of the most memorable passages of his life and times*. London: T. Parkhurst et al.

Bedwell, William (1615) *Mohammedis imposturae*. London: Richard Field.

Bellers, John (1710) *Some Reasons for an European State*. London: s.n.

Besse, Joseph (1753) *A Collection of the Sufferings of the People Called Quakers, from the Testimony of a Good Conscience, from the Time of their being First Distinguished by the Name in the Year 1650 to the Time of the Act, Commonly Called the Act of Toleration*. 2 vols. London: Luke Hinde.

Biddulph, W. (1609) *The travels of certaine Englishman*. London: W. Aspley.

Bishop, George (1661) *New England judged, not by man's, but the spirit of the Lord*. London: Robert Wilson.

Blome, Richard (1678) *A description of the island of Jamaica, with the isles and territories in America to which the English are related ... together with the present state of Algiers*. London: Dorman Newman.

Blount, Henry (1636) *A voyage into the Levant*. Second edition. London: Andrew Crooke.

Bluet, Thomas (1734) *Some memoirs of the life of Job*. London: Richard Ford.

Boulbie, Judith (1665) *A testimony for truth against all hireling priests*. London: s.n.

Bownas, Samuel (1728) *God's mercy surmounting man's cruelty, exemplified in the captivity and redemption of Elizabeth Hanson*. Philadelphia: Samuel Keimer.

Braithwaite, John (1729) *The history of the revolutions in the Empire of Morocco*. London: Darby and T. Browne.

Brooks, Francis (1693) *Barbarian cruelty being a true history of the distressed condition of the Christian captives under the tyranny of Mully Ishmael, Emperor of Morocco, and King of Fez and Macqueness in Barbary*. London: I. Salusbury and H. Newman.

Bugg, Francis (1699) *Some reasons humbly proposed to the Lords spiritual and temporal, and Commons assembled in Parliament, why the Quakers principles and practices should be examined, and censured or suppressed*. London: J. Robinson.

Bugg, Francis (1703) *Quakerism drooping, and its cause sinking*. London: C. Brome.

Burrough, Edward (1657) *The true Christian religion again discovered after the long and dark night of apostacy,* London: Giles Calvert.

Burrough, Edward (1660) *The everlasting gospel of repentance and remission of sins*. London: Robert Wilson.

Burrough, Edward (1661) *A declaration of the sad and great persecution and martyrdom of the people of God, called Quakers, in New--England for the worshipping of God.* London: Robert Wilson.

Busnot, Dominique (1715) *The history of the reign of Muley Ismael, the present king of Morocco, Fez, Tafilet, Sous, &c.* London: A. Bell.

Coxere, Edward *(1945) Adventures by sea of Edward Coxere.* E. H. W. Meyerstein (ed.). Oxford: The Clarendon Press [Originally written 1685–1694].

Croese, Gerardus (1696) *The General History of the Quakers containing the lives, tenents, sufferings, tryals, speeches and letters of the most eminent Quakers, both men and women.* London: John Dunton.

Crook, John (1662) *Truth's principles.* London: s.n.

Dan, Pierre (1646) *Histoire de Barbarie et de ses corsaires, des royaumes et des villes d'Alger, de Tunis, de Salé, et de Tripoly.* Second edition. Paris: P. Rocole.

D'Aranda, Emanuel (1666) *The history of Algiers and its slavery with many remarkable particularities of Africk.* London: John Starkey.

Davies, William (1614) *A true relation of the travailes and most miserable captivitie of William Davies, barber-surgeon of London, under the Duke of Florence.* London: Nicholas Bourne.

Deacon, John (1656) *The Grand Impostor Examined.* London: s.n.

Defoe, Daniel (1719) *The life and strange surprizing adventures of Robinson Crusoe.* London: W. Taylor.

Denham, John (1659) *A relation of a Quaker, that to the shame of his profession, attempted to bugger a mare near Colchester.* London: s.n.

Dewsbury, William (1689) *The faithful testimony of that ancient servant of the Lord, and minister of the everlasting Gospel William Dewsbery* [sic]. London: Andrew Sowle.

Dickinson, Jonathan (1699) *Jonathan Dickinson's journal of God's protecting providence.* Philadelphia: Reiner Jansen.

Digby, Kenelm (1868) *Journal of a voyage into the Mediterranean.* John Bruce (ed.). London: Camden Society [Originally written 1627–29].

Du Ryer, André (1647) *L'Alcoran de Mahomet. Translaté d'arabe en françois, par le sieur Du Ryer, sieur de la Garde Malezair.* Paris: Antoine de Somaville.

Edwards, Thomas (1647) *The casting down of the last and strongest hold of Satan. Or, A treatise against toleration and pretended liberty of conscience.* London: George Calvert.

Eigilssen, Oluf (1641). *En kort beretning om de tyrkiske Søe-Røveres onde Medfart og Omgang.* Copenhagen: s.n.

Egilsson, Ólafur (2008) *The Travels of Reverend Ólafur Egilsson (Reisbók séra Ólafs Egilssonar) Captured by Pirates in 1627.* Karl Smári Hreinsson and Adam Nichols (trans. and eds). Reykjavik: Fjölvi.

Elias, John (1674) *A true and strange relation of the travels, adventures, and great persecution of four eminent Quakers of Glocestershire who in the year 1673 travelled through France, Italy and Turkey, to promote their religion.* London: L.W.

Elias, John (1681) *A true and strange relation of the travels, adventures and great persecution of four eminent Quakers who in the year 1680, travelled through France, Italy, and Turkey, to promote their religion.* London: J. Clarke.

Ellwood, Thomas (1714) *The history of the life of Thomas Ellwood.* London: J. Sowle.

Evelyn, John (1907) *The diary of John Evelyn.* Volume 2. William Bray (ed.). London: Dent [Originally written 1641–1697].

Faldo, J. (1673) *Quakerism no Christianity.* London: Jonathan Robinson.

Farnworth, Richard (1653) *The generall-good to all people.* London: Giles Calvert.

Fell, Margaret (1655) *False Prophets, Antichrists, Deceivers.* London: Giles Calvert.

Fell, Margaret (1666) *Womens speaking justified, proved and allowed of by the Scriptures.* London: s.n.

Fell, Margaret (1668) *A call unto the seed of Israel that they may come out of Egypts darkness and house of bondage unto the land of rest.* London: Robert Wilson.

Fisher, Samuel (1660) *Rusticus ad academicos.* London: Robert Wilson.

Fox, George (1653) *Truth's defence against the refined subtilty of the serpent.* York: Tho. Wayt.

Fox, George (1654) *Several papers some of them given forth by George Fox; others by ...* London: s.n.

Fox, George (1656a) *Here all may see, that justice and judgement is to rule. And the power of God without respecting mens persons, or observing the worlds complements.* London: Thomas Simmons.

Fox, George (1656b) *The woman learning in silence: or, The mysterie of the womans subiection to her husband. As also, the daughter prophesying, wherein the Lord hath, and is fulfilling that he spake by the prophet Joel, I will poure out my spirit upon all flesh, &c.* London: Thomas Simmons.

Fox, George (1657) *Concerning good-morrow, and good-even; the worlds customs.* London: Thomas Simmons.

Fox, George (1658) *An answer to a paper which came from the papists lately out of Holland who goeth about to vindicate the Pope, Jesuits, and papists.* London: Thomas Simmons.

Fox, George (1659) *To the council of officers of the armie and the heads of the nation, and for the inferior officers and souldiers to read.* London?: s.n.

Fox, George (1660a) *Turcae, et omnibus sub ejus ditione, ut hoc perlegant quod ad salvationem eorum spectat.* London: Robert Wilson.

Fox, Geroge (1660b) *A battle-door for teachers & professors to learn singular & plural you to many, and thou to one, singular one, thou, plural many, you.* London: Robert Wilson.

Fox, George (1661a) *Concerning sons and daughters, and prophetesses speaking and prophecying*. London: M.W.

Fox, George (1661b) *Truths triumph in the eternal power over the darke inventions of fallen man*. London: Thomas Simmons.

Fox, George (1664) *For all the bishops and priests in Christendom*. Worcester : s.n.

Fox, George (1667a) *Something in answer to a book called Fiat Lux*. London: s.n.

Fox, George (1667b) *Something in answer to Lodowick Muggleton's book, which he calls The Quaker's neck broken wherein, in judging others he hath judged himself*. London: s.n.

Fox, George (1671) *The heathen's divinity set upon the heads of all called Christians*. London: s.n.

Fox, George (1672) *To the ministers, teachers, and priests (so called and so stileing your selves) in Barbadoes*. London: s.n.

Fox, George (1673) *An epistle to all professors in New-England, Germany, and other parts of the called Christian world also to the Jews and Turks throughout the world, that they may see who are the true worshippers of God, that He seeks, and in what He is worshipped ...* London?: s.n.

Fox, George (1674) *A warning to England and to all that profess themselves Christians, who have the form, but deny the power of godliness, that they sin no more, lest a worse thing come to them*. London: s.n.

Fox, George (1676) *Concerning the true baptism and the false*. London: s.n.

Fox, George (1677) *The hypocrites fast and feast not God's holy day. Hat-honour to men man's institution not God's*. London: s.n.

Fox, George (1680) *To the Great Turk and his King at Argiers together with a postscript of George Pattison's taking the Turks and setting them on their own shoar*. London: Ben Clark.

Fox, George (1685) *A distinction betwixt the two suppers of Christ*. London: s.n.

Fox, George (1688) *An answer to the speech or decalration [sic] of the great Turk, Sulton [sic] Mahomet ... This was written, by George Fox, five years since, being 1683 and is it now a true prophesie, and fulfilled on the Great Turk Sulan Mahomet who was removed and put out of his high throne the year 1687*. London: A. Sowle.

Fox, George (1694) *A Journal or historical account of the life, travels, sufferings, Christian experiences and labour of love in the work of the ministry, of ... George Fox*. Thomas Ellwood (ed.). London: Thomas Northcott.

Fox, George (1698) *A collection of many select and Christian epistles, letters and testimonies written on sundry occasions, by that ancient, eminent, faithful friend and minister of Christ Jesus, George Fox*. London: T. Sowle.

Fox, George (1706) *Gospel-truth demonstrated, in a collection of doctrinal books, given forth by that faithful minister of Jesus Christ, George Fox: containing principles, essential to Christianity and salvation, held among the people called Quakers*. London: T. Sowle.

Fox, George (1831) *The Works of George Fox.* 8 vols. Philadelphia: Marcus T. C. Gould.

Fox George (1911) *The Journal of George Fox.* 2 vols. Penney, Norman (ed.). Cambridge: Cambridge University Press.

Fox, George (1952) *Journal of George Fox.* John L. Nickalls (ed.). Cambridge: Cambridge University Press.

Fox, George (2000 [1948]) *George Fox's 'Book of Miracles'.* Henry J. Cadbury (ed.). Second edition. Philadelphia: Friends General Conference.

Fox, George and Nayler, James (1653) *Saul's errand to Damascus.* London: Giles Calvert.

Furly, Benjamin (1663) *The worlds honour detected, and, for the unprofitableness thereof, rejected.* London: Robert Wilson.

Gaskin, John (1660) *A just defence and vindication of gospel ministers and gospel ordinances against the Quakers many false accusations, slanders and reproaches.* London: W.G.

Gilpin, John (1655) *The Quakers shaken, or, a warning against quaking.* London: Simon Waterson.

Hanmer, Meredith (1586) *The baptizing of a Turke.* London: Robert Walde-graue.

Higginson, F. (1653) A *brief relation of the irreligion of the northern Quakers.* London: H.R.

Howgill, Francis (1655) *The common salvation contended for, and the faith which was once delivered to the saints.* London: Giles Calvert.

Hubberthorn, Richard (1654) *The testimony of the everlasting gospel witnessed through sufferings.* Norwich?: s.n.

Hubberthorn, Richard (1660) *Something that lately passed in discourse between the King and R.H. published to prevent the mistakes and errors in a copy lately printed contrary to the knowledge or intention of the party concerned.* London: Giles Calvert.

Keith, George (1674) *An account of the oriental philosophy shewing the wisdom of some renowned men of the east and particularly the profound wisdom of Hai Ebn Yokdan.* London: s.n.

Keith, George (1693) *An exhortation & caution to Friends concerning buying or keeping of Negroes.* New York: William Bradford.

Keith, George (1702) *The standard of the Quakers examined.* London: Aylmer.

Knolles, Richard (1603) *The generall historie of the Turkes.* London: Adam Islip.

Knox, Robert (1681) *An historical relation of the island Ceylon in the East Indies.* London: Richard Chiswell.

Leslie, Charles (1696) *The snake in the grass.* London: Charles Brome.

Leslie, Charles (1698) *A short and easie method with the Deists.* London: John Reid.

Lithgow, W. (1623) *A most delectable and true discourse of an admired and painefnll [sic] peregrination from Scotland.* London: Nicholas Okes.

London Yearly Meeting (1858) *Epistles from the Yearly Meeting of Friends held in London ... from 1681 to 1857.* Volume One. London: E. Marsh.

Lurting, Thomas (1710) *The fighting sailor turn'd peaceable Christian.* London: J. Sowle.

Moryson, F. (1617) *An itinerary vvritten by Fynes Moryson gent.* London: Thomas Archer.

North, R. (1744) *The life of the Honourable Sir Dudley North.* London: John Whiston.

Okeley, William (1684 [1675]) *Eben-ezer, or, A small monument of great mercy appearing in miraculous deliverance of William Okeley, William Adams, John Anthony, John Jephs, John Carpenter, from the miserable slavery of Algiers, with the wonderful means of their escape in a boat of canvas.* London: Nat. Ponder.

Pellow, Thomas (1739) *The history of the long captivity and adventures of Thomas Pellow, in South Barbary.* London: R. Goadby.

Penington, Isaac (1661) *Some questions and answers for the opening of the eyes of the Jews natural that they may see the hope of Israel which hath so long been hid from them.* London: Robert Wilson.

Penn, William (1669) *No cross, no crown, or, Several sober reasons against hat-honour, titular-respects, you to a single person, with the apparel and recreations of the times being inconsistant with Scripture.* London: s.n.

Penn, William (1672) *The spirit of truth vindicated, against that of error & envy unseasonably manifested.* London: s.n.

Penn, William (1693) *An essay towards the present and future peace of Europe by the establishment of an European dyet, parliament, or estates.* London: Randal Taylor.

Pepys, Samuel (2003) *The Diaries of Samuel Pepys – A Selection.* Robert Latham (ed.). Second edition. London: Penguin Classics [Originally written 1660–1669].

Perrot, John (1656) *A visitation of love and gentle greeting of the Turk and tender tryal of his thoughts for God.* London: Thomas Simmons.

Perrot, John (1661) *Blessed openings of a day of good things to the Turks written to the heads, rulers, ancients, and elders of their land, and whomsoever else it may concern.* London: Thomas Simmons.

Pitts, Joseph (1704) *A true and faithful account of the religion and manners of the Mohammetans.* Exeter: S. Farley.

Pitts, Joseph (1731) *A faithful account of the religion and manners of the Mohammetans.* Third edition. London: Osborn and Longman.

Pococke, Edward (1650) *Specimen historiae arabum.* Oxford: H. Hall.

Poole, Josua (1657) *The English Parnassus.* London: Thomas Johnson.

Prideaux, Humphrey (1697) *The true nature of imposture fully display'd in the life of Mahomet with a discourse annexed for the vindicating of Christianity from this charge: offered to the consideration of the deists of the present age.* London: William Rogers.

Rawlins, John (1622) *The famous and wonderfull recoverie of a ship of Bristoll, called the Exchange, from the Turkish pirates of Argier.* London: Nathaniel Butler.

Rolamb [sic], Claes (1732) 'A relation of a Journey to Constantinople.' In *A collection of voyages and travels, some now first printed from original manuscripts, others now first published in English.* Volume 5. London: Churchill, pp. 671–716.

Rosee, Pascha (1666) *The vertue of the coffee drink.* London: s.n.

Ross, Alexander (1649) *The Alcoran of Mahomet, translated out of Arabique into French; by the sieur Du Ryer, Lord of Malezair, and resident for the King of France, at Alexandria. And newly Englished, for the satisfaction of all that desire to look into the Turkish vanities.* London: s.n.

Sale, George (1734) *The Koran, commonly called the Alcoran of Mohammed, translated into English immediately from the original Arabic; with explanatory notes.* London: C. Ackers.

Sewel, William (1722) *The history of the rise, increase, and progress of the Christian people called Quakers.* 2 vols. London: J. Sowle.

Smith, Henry (1593) *Gods arrowe against atheists.* London: John Danter.

Smith, Stephen (1676) *Wholsome advice and information.* London: s.n.

Smith, Stephen (1679) *The true light discovered.* London: s.n.

Spratt, Devereux (1886) *Autobiography of the Rev. D. Spratt, who died at Mitchelstown, Co. Cork, 1688.* Thomas Abel Bremage Spratt (ed.). London: Taylor and Hudson.

Stubbe, Henry (1659) *A light shining out of darknes ... with a brief apologie for the Quakers, that they are not inconsistent with a magistracy.* London: s.n.

Stubbe, Henry (1911) *An account of the rise and progress of Mahometanism with the life of Mahomet and a vindication of him and his religion from the calumnies of the Christians.* Hafiz Shairani (ed.). London: Luzac [Originally written 1673–1676].

T. B. (1672) *A journey to Jerusalem.* London: Nathaniel Crouch.

T[homas] S[mith] (1670) *The adventures of (Mr. T.S.) an English merchant taken prisoner by the Turks of Argiers.* London: Moses Pitt.

Thurloe, John (1742) *A Collection of the State Papers of John Thurloe Esq. Secretary first, to the Council of State, and afterwards to the two Protectors, Oliver and Richard Cromwell. In seven volumes. Containing Authentic Memorials of the English Affairs from the Year 1638, to the Restoration of King Charles II.* Volume Seven. London: Fletcher Gyles.

White, Thomas and Dury, John (1659) *A true relation of the conversion and baptism of Isuf the Turkish Chaous, named Richard Christophilus In the presence of a full congregation, Jan. 30. 1658. in Covent-Garden, where Mr. Manton is minister.* London: S. Griffin.

Wilson, Elias (1673) *Strange and wonderful news from Italy.* London: John Lock.

Wright, James (1684) *The history and antiquities of the County of Rutland collected from records, ancient manuscripts, monuments on the place, and other authorities: illustrated with sculptures.* London: Bennet Griffin.

Secondary Texts

Ådahl, Karin (ed.) (2006) *The Sultan's Procession: The Swedish Embassy to Sultan Mehmed IV in 1657–1658 and the Rålamb Paintings.* London: Swedish Research Institute in Istanbul.

Ahmad, Aijaz (1992) 'Orientalism and After: Ambivalence and Cosmopolitan Location in the Work of Edward Said.' *Economic and Political Weekly,* 27.30: 98–116.

Akbari, Suzanne C. (2009) *Idols in the East: European Representations of Islam and the Orient, 1100–1450.* Ithaca: Cornell University Press.

Al-Ahari, Muhammad A. (ed.). (2006) *Five Classic Muslim Slave Narratives.* Chicago: Magribine Press.

Al-Azmeh, Aziz (1991) *Arabs and Barbarians: Medieval Arabic Ethnology and Ethnography* [in Arabic]. London: Riad El-Rayyes.

Al-Azmeh, Aziz (1992) 'Barbarians in Arab Eyes.' *Past & Present,* 134: 3–18.

Allen, R. C. (2003) '"Mocked, scoffed, persecuted, and made a gazeing stock": The resistance of the Religious Society of Friends (Quakers) to the religious and civil authorities in post-toleration south-east Wales c.1689–1836.' *Cycnos,* 19.1: 23–47.

Andrea, Bernadette (2007) *Women and Islam in Early Modern Literature.* Cambridge: Cambridge University Press.

Andrews, Charles McLean (1942) 'God's Protecting Providence: A Journal by Jonathan Dickinson.' *The Florida Historical Quarterly,* 21.2: 107–126.

Andrews, Charles Mclean and Andrews, Evangeline Walker (eds.) (1945) *Jonathan Dickinson's Journal or, God's Protecting Providence. Being the Narrative of a Journey from Port Royal in Jamaica to Philadelphia between August 23, 1696 to April 1, 1697.* New Haven: Yale University Press.

Ashcroft, Bill and Ahluwalia, Pal (2001) *Edward Said.* Third edition. London: Routledge.

Auchterlonie, Paul (2012) *Encountering Islam. Joseph Pitts: An English Slave in 17th-Century Algiers and Mecca.* London: Arabian Publishing.

Aylmer, G. E. (1999) 'Slavery under Charles II: the Mediterranean and Tangier.' *English Historical Review,* 114: 378–388.

Ayoub, R. (2005) 'The Persecution of "an Innocent People" in Seventeenth-Century England.' *Quaker Studies,* 10: 46–66.

Baer, Marc D. (2008) *Honored by the Glory of Islam: Conversion and Conquest in Ottoman Europe.* New York: Oxford University Press.

Baker, Naomi (2001) '"Men of our own Nation": Gender, Race and the Other in Early Modern Quaker Writing.' *Literature & History,* 10: 1–25.

Ball, B. (1975) *A Great Expectation: Eschatological Thought in English Protestantism to 1660.* Leiden: Brill.

Barbour, Hugh (1964) *The Quakers in Puritan England.* New Haven: Yale University Press.

Barbour, Hugh and Arthur O. Roberts (2004) *Early Quaker Writings, 1650–1700.* Second edition. Wallingford: Pendle Hill Publications.

Barletta, Vincent (2010) *Death in Babylon: Alexander the Great and Iberian Empire in the Muslim Orient*. Chicago: University of Chicago Press.

Bauman, Richard (1983) *Let Your Words Be Few: Symbolism of Speaking and Silence among Seventeenth-Century Quakers*. Cambridge: Cambridge University Press.

Beckingham, C. F. (1950) 'The Date of Pitts's Pilgrimage to Mecca.' *Journal of the Royal Asiatic Society*, 82: 112–113.

Benhayoun, Jamal Eddine (2006) *Narration, Navigation, and Colonialism: A Critical Account of Seventeenth- and Eighteenth-Century English Narratives of Adventure and Captivity*. Brussels: P.I.E. Peter Lang.

Bennassar, Bartolomé and Bennassar, Lucile (2006) *Les chrétiens d'Allah: l'histoire extraordinaire des renégats XVIe Et XVIIe siècles*. Paris: Perrin.

Bent, J. Theodore (1890) 'The English in the Levant.' *The English Historical Review*, 5.20: 654–664.

Bent, J. Theodore (ed.) (1893) *Early Voyages and Travels in the Levant*. London: Hakluyt Society.

Birchwood, Matthew (2005) 'News from Vienna: Titus Oates and the True Protestant Turks.' In Matthew Birchwood and Matthew Dimmock (eds), *Cultural Encounters Between East and West, 1453–1699*. Newcastle: Cambridge Scholars Press, pp. 64–76.

Birchwood, Matthew (2007) '"Vindicating The Prophet": Universal Monarchy and Henry Stubbe's biography of Mohammed.' *Prose Studies*, 29.1: 59–72.

Birchwood, Matthew and Matthew Dimmock (2005) 'Introduction.' In Matthew Birchwood and Matthew Dimmock (eds), *Cultural Encounters Between East and West, 1453–1699*. Newcastle: Cambridge Scholars Press, pp. 1–9.

Bisaha, Nancy (2006) *Creating East and West: Renaissance Humanists and the Ottoman Turks*. Philadelphia: University of Pennsylvania Press.

Bitterman, M. G. F. (1973) 'The Early Quaker Literature of Defense.' *Church History*, 42.2: 203–228.

Bittle, William G. (1986) *James Nayler 1618–1660: The Quaker Indicted by Parliament*. York: William Sessions.

Blackmore, Josiah (2009) *Moorings: Portuguese Expansion and the Writing of Africa*. Minneapolis: University of Minnesota Press.

Blanks, David R. and Michael Frassetto (1999) *Western Views of Islam in Medieval and Early Modern Europe: Perception of Other*. London: Palgrave MacMillan.

Blunt, Wilfrid (1951) *Black Sunrise: the Life and Times of Mulai Ismail, Emperor of Morocoo, 1646–1727*. London: Methuen.

Bobzin, Hartmut (1985) 'Martin Luthers Beitrag zur Kenntnis und Kritik des Islam.' *Neue Zeitschrift für Systematische Theologie*, 27: 262– 289.

Bolster, W. J. (1998) *Black Jacks: African American Seamen in the Age of Sail*. Second edition. Cambridge: Harvard University Press.

Braithwaite, William C. (1955) *The Beginnings of Quakerism.* Second edition. Cambridge: Cambridge University Press.

Braithwaite, William C. (1979) *The Second Period of Quakerism.* Second edition. York: William Sessions.

Braudel, Fernand (1972) *Mediterranean and the Mediterranean World in the Age of Philip II.* 2 vols. London: Collins.

Brecht, Martin (2000) 'Luther und die Türken.' In Bodo Guthmüller and Wilhelm Kühlmann (eds), *Europa und die Türken in der Renaissance.* Tübingen: Niemeyer, pp. 9–27.

Briggs, Asa, and Peter Burke (2010) *Social History of the Media: From Gutenberg to the Internet.* Cambridge: Polity.

Brooks, J. F., C. R. N. DeCorse, and J. Walton (eds) (2009) *Small Worlds: Method, Meaning, & Narrative in Microhistory.* Santa Fe: SAR Press.

Brown, Sylvia. (2007) 'The Radical Travels of Mary Fisher: Walking and Writing in the Universal Light.' In Sylvia Brown (ed.), *Women, Gender and Radical Religion in Early Modern Europe.* Leiden: Brill, pp. 39–64.

Bruyneel, Sally (2010) *Margaret Fell and the End of Time.* Waco: Baylor University Press.

Burgess, S. M. and E. Maas (eds) (2002) *The New International Dictionary of Pentecostal and Charismatic Movements.* Grand Rapids: Zondervan.

Burman, Thomas E. (2007) *Reading the Qur'an in Latin Christendom, 1140–1560.* Philadelphia: University of Pennsylvania Press.

Burton, Jonathan (2005) *Traffic and Turning: Islam and English Drama, 1579–1624.* Newark: University of Delaware Press.

Butler, D. M. (1999) *The Quaker Meeting Houses of Britain.* Volume 2. London: Friends Historical Society.

Cadbury, Henry J. (ed.) (1939) *Annual Catalogue of George Fox's Papers, Compiled in 1694–1697.* Philadelphia: Friends Book Store.

Cadbury, Henry J. (1952) 'George Fox's Later Years.' In John J. Nickalls, *Journal of George Fox.* Cambridge: Cambridge University Press, pp. 713–760.

Cadbury, Henry J. (ed.) (1972) *Narrative Papers of George Fox, Unpublished or Uncollected. Edited from the Manuscripts with Introductions and Notes.* Richmond: Friends United Press.

Cadbury, Henry J. (1974) 'Friends and the Inquisition at Malta.' *Journal of the Friends' Historical Society,* 53: 219–225.

Campbell, Mary B. (1993) *The Witness and the Other World: Exotic European Travel Writing, 400–1600.* Ithaca: Cornell University Press.

Campi, E. (2010) 'Early Reformed attitudes towards Islam.' *Theological Review of the Near East School of Theology,* 31.2: 131–151.

Cantor, Geoffrey (2005) *Quakers, Jews, and Science Religious Responses to Modernity and the Sciences in Britain, 1650–1900.* Oxford: Oxford University Press.

Capp, Bernard (1972) *The Fifth Monarchy Men.* London: Faber and Faber.

Capp, Bernard (1979) *Astrology and the Popular Press: English Almanacs 1500–1800*. London: Faber.

Carboni, Stefano (ed.) (2007) *Venice and the Islamic World, 828–1797*. New Haven: Yale University Press.

Cardini, Franco (2001) *Europe and Islam*. Oxford: Wiley-Blackwell.

Carey, Brycchan (2010) 'Inventing a Culture of Antislavery: Pennsylvania Quakers and the Germantown Protest of 1688.' In Cora Kaplan and John Oldfield (eds), *Imagining Transatlantic Slavery and Abolition*. Basingstoke: Palgrave Macmillan, pp. 17–32.

Carey, Brycchan (2012) *From Peace to Freedom: Quaker Rhetoric and the Birth of American Antislavery, 1657–1761*. New Haven: Yale University Press.

Carey, Daniel and Claire Jowitt (2009) 'Early Modern Travel Writing: Varieties, Transitions, Horizons.' *Studies in Travel Writing*, 13:2: 95–192.

Carey, Daniel and Claire Jowitt (eds) (2012) *Richard Hakluyt and Travel Writing in Early Modern Europe*. Aldershot: Ashgate.

Carroll, Kenneth (1971) *John Perrot: Early Quaker schismatic*. London: Friends' Historical Society.

Carrroll, Kenneth (1978) 'Early Quakers and "Going Naked As A Sign".' *Quaker History*, 67: 69–87.

Carrroll, Kenneth (1982) 'Quaker Slaves in Algiers, 1679–1688.' *Journal of the Friends' Historical Society*, 54.7: 301–12.

Carroll, Kenneth L. (1985) 'A look at James Milner and his "false prophecy."' *Quaker History*, 74.1: 18–26.

Carroll, Kenneth (1985–1986) 'Quaker Captives in Morocco, 1685–1701.' *Journal of the Friends' Historical Society*, 55.3–4: 67–79.

Carroll, Kenneth (2008) 'Early Quakers and Fasting.' *Quaker History*, 97.1: 1–10.

Carroll, Kenneth (2010) 'Persecution and Persecutors of Maryland Quakers, 1658–1661.' *Quaker History*, 99.1: 15–31.

Castries, Henry de (1928) 'Trois Princes Marocains, Convertis Au Christianisme.' In *Mémorial Henri Basset: nouvelles études nord-africaines et orientales*. Volume 1. Paris: L'Institut des hautes-études marocaines, pp. 141–158.

Cesare, Michelina Di (2012) *The Pseudo-historical Image of the Prophet Muhammad in Medieval Latin Literature: A Repertory*. Berlin: Walter de Gruyter.

Champion, Justin A. I. (1999) 'Apocrypha, canon and criticism from Samuel Fisher to John Toland, 1650–1718.' In A. P. Coudert, S. Hutton, R. H. Popkin, and G. M. Weiner (eds), *Judaeo-Christian Intellectual Culture in the Seventeenth Century: A Celebration of the Library of Narcissus Marsh (1638–1713)*. Dordrecht: Kluwer, pp. 91–117.

Chappell, E. (ed.) (1935) *The Tangiers Papers of Samuel Pepys*. London: Navy Records Society.

Ciappara, Frans (2004) 'Christendom and Islam: A Fluid Frontier.' *Mediterranean Studies*, 13: 165–187.

Çirakman, Asli (2002) *From the 'Terror of the World' to the 'Sick Man of Europe': European Images of Ottoman Empire and Society from the Sixteenth Century to the Nineteenth*. New York: Peter Lang.

Clarence-Smith, William Gervase (2006) *Islam and the Abolition of Slavery*. Oxford: Oxford University Press.

Coffey, J. (2000) *Persecution and Toleration in Protestant England, 1558–1689*. Harlow: Longman.

Colish, M. L. (2009) 'Juan Luis Vives on the Turks.' *Medievalia et Humanistica*, 35: 1–14.

Colley, Linda (2002) *Captives: Britain, the Empire and the World*. London: Jonathan Cape.

Colombo, Emanuele (2011) 'Baldassarre Loyola De Mandes (1631–1667), Prince De Fez et Jésuite.' In Jocelyne Dakhlia and Bernard Vincent (eds), *Les musulmans dans l'histoire de l'Europe: Tome 1, Une intégration invisible*. Paris: Albin Michel, pp. 159–193.

Cook, David (2005) *Contemporary Muslim Apocalyptic Literature*. Syracuse: Syracuse University Press.

Corns, T. and D. Loewenstein (eds) (1996) *The Emergence of Quaker Writing: Dissenting Literature in Seventeenth-Century England*. Second edition. London: Routledge.

Curtin, Philip (1969) *The Atlantic Slave Trade: A Census*. Second edition. Madison: University of Wisconsin Press.

Dakhlia, Jocelyne and Bernard Vincent (eds). (2011) *Les musulmans dans l'histoire de l'Europe*. Paris: Albin Michel.

Daniel, Norman (1993) *Islam and the West: The Making of an Image*. Second edition. Oxford: Oneworld.

Davis, Robert C. (2001) 'Counting European Slaves on the Barbary Coast.' *Past & Present*, 172: 87–124.

Davis, Robert C. (2004) *Christian slaves, Muslim masters. White Slavery in the Mediterranean, the Barbary Coast, and Italy, 1500–1800*. Basingstoke: Palgrave Macmillan.

Davis, Robert C. (2009) *Holy War and Human Bondage: Tales of Christian-Muslim Slavery in the Early-Modern Mediterranean*. Santa Barbara: Praeger.

Davies, Adrian (2000) *The Quakers in English Society, 1655–1725*. Oxford: Clarendon Press.

Davies, S. (1998) *Unbridled Spirits: Women of the English Revolution, 1640–1660*. London: Women's Press.

Damrosch, Leopold (1996) *The Sorrows of the Quaker Jesus: James Nayler and the Puritan Crackdown on the Free Spirit*. Cambridge: Harvard University Press.

Dimmock, Matthew (2005) *New Turkes: Dramatizing Islam and The Ottomans In Early Modern England*. Farnham: Ashgate.

Dimmock, Matthew (2013) *Mythologies of the Prophet Muhammad in Early Modern English Culture*. Cambridge: Cambridge University Press.

Driessen, Henk (1992) *On the Spanish-Moroccan Frontier: A Study in Ritual Power and Ethnicity.* Oxford: Berg.

Dursteler, Eric R. (2011) *Renegade Women: Gender, Identity, and Boundaries in the Early Modern Mediterranean.* Baltimore: The Johns Hopkins University Press.

Eckhardt, A. (1949) 'Le cercueil flottant de Mahomet', in *Mélanges de philologie romane et de littérature médiévale offerts à Ernest Hoepffner.* Paris: Les Belles Lettres, pp. 77–88.

Eeg-Olofsson, Leif (1954) *The Conception of the Inner Light in Robert Barclay's Theology: A Study in Quakerism.* Lund: C.W.K. Gleerup.

Ehmann, Johannes (2008) *Luther, Türken und Islam: Eine Untersuchung zum Türken- und Islambild Martin Luthers (1515–1546).* Gütersloh: Gütersloher Verlag.

Elmarsafy, Ziad (2009a) 'Philosophy Self-Taught: Reason, Mysticism and the Uses of Islam in the Early Enlightenment.' In Mercedes Garcia-Arenal, Benard Heyberger, Emanuele Colombo and Vismara Paola (eds), *L'Islam visto da Occidente: Cultura e religione del Seicento europeo di fronte all'Islam.* Genoa and Milan: Marietti, pp. 135–155.

Elmarsafy, Ziad (2009b) *The Enlightenment Qur'an: The Politics of Translation and the Construction of Islam.* Oxford: Oneworld.

Elmer, Peter (1996) "Saints or Sorcerers": Quakerism, Demonology and the Decline of Witchcraft in Seventeenth-Century England.' In Jonathan Barry, Marianne Hester and Gareth Roberts (eds), *Witchcraft in Early Modern Europe: Studies in Culture and Belief.* Cambridge: Cambridge University Press, pp. 145–179.

Endy, M. B. (1981) 'The Interpretation of Quakerism: Rufus Jones and His Critics.' *Quaker History*, 70:1, 3–21.

Eysturlid, Lee W. (1993) 'Where Everything Is Weighed in the Scales of Material Interest: Anglo-Turkish Trade, Piracy and Diplomacy in the Mediterranean During the Jacobean Period.' *Journal of European Economic History*, 22: 613–626.

Fichtner, Paula Sutter (2008) *Terror and Toleration: The Habsburg Empire Confronts Islam, 1526–1850.* London: Reaktion Books.

Fisher, David Hackett. (1989) *Albion's Seed: Four British Folkways in America.* Oxford: Oxford University Press.

Frampton, T. L. (2007) *Spinoza and the Rise of Historical Criticism of the Bible.* London: Continuum.

Francisco, Adam S. (2007) *Martin Luther and Islam: A Study in Sixteenth-Century Polemics and Apologetics.* Leiden: Brill.

Frampton, T. L. (2007) *Spinoza and the Rise of Historical Criticism of the Bible.* London: Continuum International Publishing Group.

Fried, J. (2004) *Les fruits de l'Apocalypse: Origines de la penseé scientifique moderne au Moyen Age.* Paris: Les éditions de la Maison des sciences de l'homme.

Friedman, Ellen G. (1983) *Spanish Captives in North Africa in the Early Modern Age.* Madison: The University of Wisconsin Press.

Garces, Maria Antonia (ed.) (2011) *An Early Modern Dialogue with Islam: Antonio de Sosa's Topography of Algiers (1612).* Chicago: University of Notre Dame Press.

Garcia, Humberto (2011) 'Turning Turk, Turning Heretic of Exeter and the Early Enlightenment, 1640–1740.' In Gerald MacLean (ed.), *Britain and the Muslim World: Historical Perspectives.* Newcastle: Cambridge Scholars Press, pp. 85–101.

Gdoura, Wahid (1985) *Le debut de l'imprimerie arabe a Istanbul et en Syrie: evolution de l'environnement culturel* (1706–1787). Tunis: L'Institut supérieur de documentation.

Gencer, Yasmin (2010) 'Ibrahim Müteferrika and the Age of the Printed Manuscript.' In Christiane J. Gruber (ed.), *The Islamic Manuscript Tradition: Ten Centuries of Book Arts in Indiana University Collections.* Bloomington: Indiana University Press, pp. 154–194.

George-Tvrtkovic, Rita (2007) *The Ambivalence of Interreligious Experience: Riccoldo da Monte Croce's Theology of Islam.* Unpublished PhD Thesis: University of Notre Dame.

George-Tvrtkovic, Rita (2013) *A Christian Pilgrim in Medieval Iraq: Riccoldo Da Montecroce's Encounter with Islam.* Begijnhof: Brepols.

Gerbner, Katharine (2007) 'We are Against the Traffik of Mens-Body: The Germantown Quaker Protest of 1688 and the Origins of American Abolitionism.' *Pennsylvania History*, 74.2: 149–172.

Goddard, Hugh (2000) *A History of Muslim-Christian Relations.* Edinburgh: Edinburgh University Press.

Goffman, Daniel (2002) *The Ottoman Empire and Early Modern Europe.* Cambridge: Cambridge University Press.

Goldish, Matt (2004) *The Sabbatean Prophets.* Cambridge: Harvard University Press.

Gow, Andrew Colin (1995) *The Red Jews: Antisemitism in an Apocalyptic Age 1200–1600.* Leiden: Brill.

Gragg, L. D. (2009) *The Quaker Community on Barbados: Challenging the Culture of the Planter Class.* Columbia: University of Missouri Press.

Grassby, R. (1994) *The English Gentleman in Trade: The Life and Works of Sir Dudley North, 1641–1691.* Oxford: Oxford University Press.

Greaves, Richard L. (1992) 'Shattered Expectations? George Fox, the Quakers, and the Restoration State, 1660–1685.' *Albion*, 24.2: 237–259.

Gribben, Crawford (2000) *The Puritan Millennium: Literature and Theology, 1550–1682.* Dublin: Four Courts Press.

Grigg, David (1980) *Population Growth and Agrarian Change: An Historical Perspective.* Cambridge: Cambridge University Press.

Guibbory, Achsah (2001) 'Conversation, Conversion, Messianic Redemption: Margaret Fell, Menasseh ben Israel, and the Jews.' In Claude J. Summer and Ted-Larry Pebworth (eds), *Literary Circles and Cultural Communities in Renaissance England.* Columbia: University of Missouri Press, pp. 210–234.

Guiton, G. (2012) *The Early Quakers and 'the Kingdom of God'*. San Francisco: Inner Light Books.

Gummere, Amelia Mott (1908) *Witchcraft And Quakerism: A Study In Social History*. London: Headley Bros.

Gwyn, Douglas (1986) *Apocalypse of the Word: the Life and Message of George Fox (1624–1691)*. Richmond: Friends United Press.

Hall, Bruce (2005) 'The Question of "Race" in the Pre-colonial Southern Sahara.' *Journal of North African Studies*, 10.3–4: 339–67.

Hall, John R. (2009) *Apocalypse: From Antiquity to the Empire of Modernity*. Cambridge: Polity.

Hamm, T. D. (1993) 'George Fox and the politics of late nineteenth-century Quaker historiography.' In Michael Mullett (ed.), *New light on George Fox* (1624 to 1691). York: Sessions, pp. 11–21.

Harper, James G. (ed.) (2011) *The Turk and Islam in the Western Eye, 1450–1750*. London: Ashgate.

Haug-Moritz, Gabriele and Ludolf Pelizaeus (eds) (2010) *Repräsentationen der islamischen Welt im Europa der Frühen Neuzeit*. Münster: Aschendorff.

Helgason, þorsteinn (1995) 'Hverjir voru Tyrkjaránsmenn?' *Saga*, 33: 110–134.

Helgason, þorsteinn (1997) 'Historical Narratives as Collective Therapy: the case of the Turkish raid in Iceland.' *Scandinavian Journal of History*, 22: 275–289.

Hertel, R. and S. Schuelting (eds) (2012) *Early Modern Encounters with the Islamic East – Performing Cultures*. Aldershot: Ashgate.

Hessayon, A. and D. Finnegan (2011) 'Introduction: Reappraising early modern radicals and radicalism.' In Ariel Hessayon and David Finnegan (eds), *Varieties of Seventeenth- and early Eighteenth-century English Radicalism in Context*. Aldershot: Ashgate, pp. 1–29.

Heyberger, B., M. Garcia-Arenal, E. Colombo, and P. Vismara (eds) (2009) *L'Islam visto da Occidente: cultura e religione del Seicento europeo di fronte all'islam; atti del convegno internazionale, Milano, Università degli studi, 17–18 ottobre 2007*. Genova: Marietti.

Hill, Christopher (1972) *The World Turned Upside Down: Radical Ideas During the English Revolution*. London: Maurice Temple Smith.

Hill, Christopher (1984) *The Experience of Defeat: Milton and Some Contemporaries*. New York: Viking Penguin.

Hill, Christopher (1990) *A Nation of Change and Novelty: Radical Politics, Religion and Literature in Seventeenth-Century England*. London: Routledge.

Hill, Christopher (1993) *The English Bible and the Seventeenth-Century Revolution*. Harmondsworth: Penguin.

Hinds, Hilary (2011) *George Fox and Early Quaker Culture*. Manchester: Manchester University Press.

Hitchcock, Richard (2008) *Mozarabs in Medieval and Early Modern Spain: Identities and Influences*. Farnham: Ashgate.

Höfert, Almut (2000) 'The Order of Things and the Discourses of the Turkish Threat: The Conceptualisation of Islam in the Rise of Occidental Anthropology in the Fifteenth and Sixteenth Centuries.' In Almut Höfert and Armando Salvatore (eds), *Between Europe and Islam: Shaping Modernity in a Transcultural Space*. Brussels: European Interuniversity Press, pp. 39–70.

Höfert, Almut (2003a) *Den Feind beschreiben: "Türkengefahr" und europäisches Wissen über das Osmanische Reich 1450–1600*. Campus: Frankfurt am Main.

Höfert, Almut (2003b) 'Ist das Böse schmutzig? Das Osmanische Reich in den Augen europäischer Beobachter des 15. und 16. Jahrhunderts.' *Historische Anthropologie*, 11: 176–192.

Höfert, Almut (2007) 'Europe and Religion in the Framework of Sixteenth-Century Relations between Christian Powers and the Ottoman Empire.' In Hans-Åke Persson and Bo Stråth (eds), *Reflections on Europe: Defining a Political Order in Time and Space*. Brussels: European Interuniversity Press, pp. 211–230.

Holmberg, Eva Johanna (2007) 'Esthers in the Seraglio: Jewish Women in Early Modern English Travel Narratives on Turkey.' In Anu Korhonen and Kate Lowe (eds), *The Trouble with Ribs: Women, Men and Gender in Early Modern Europe*. Helsinki: Helsinki Collegium for Advanced Studies, pp. 34–56.

Holt, P. M. (1972) *A Seventeenth-Century Defender of Islam: Henry Stubbe (1632–76) and his Book*. London: Dr William's Trust.

Horle, C. W. (1988) *The Quakers and the English Legal System 1660–1688*. Philadelphia: University of Pennsylvania Press.

Hourani, Albert (1992) *Islam in European Thought*. Cambridge: Cambridge University Press.

Hughes, Derek (2007) *Versions of Blackness: Key Texts on Slavery from the Seventeenth Century*. Cambridge: Cambridge University Press.

Hulsebosch, D. J. (2006) 'Nothing But Liberty: Somerset's Case and the British Empire.' *Law and History Review*, 24.3: 647–658.

Humberto, Garcia (2011) 'Turning Turk, Turning Heretic: Joseph Pitts of Exeter and the Early Enlightenment, 1640–1740.' In Gerald MacLean (ed.), *Britain and the Muslim World: Historical Perspectives*. Newcastle: Cambridge Scholars, pp. 85–101.

Ingle, H. Larry (1987) 'From Mysticism to Radicalism: Recent Historiography of Quaker Beginnings.' *Quaker History*, 76: 79–94.

Ingle, H. Larry (1992) 'George Fox, Millenarian.' *Albion*, 24: 261–278.

Ingle, H. Larry (1994) *First Among Friends: George Fox and the Creation of Quakerism*. Oxford: Oxford University Press.

Jacob, J. R. (1983) *Henry Stubbe, Radical Protestantism and the early Enlightenment*. Cambridge: Cambridge University Press.

Jamieson, Alan G. (2012) *Lords of the Sea: A History of the Barbary Corsairs*. London: Reaktion Books.

Jayyusi, Salma Khadra (ed.) (1994) *The Legacy of Muslim Spain*. Leiden: Brill.

Johnston, Warren (2011) *Revelation Restored: The Apocalypse in Later Seventeenth-Century England*. Woodbridge: Boydell Press.

Jones, T. Canby (1984) *George Fox's Attitude Toward War*. Richmond: Friends United Press.

Jónsson, Már (2007) 'The expulsion of the Moriscos from Spain in 1609–1614: the destruction of an Islamic periphery.' *Journal of Global History*, 2: 195–212.

Joyner, Charles W. (1999) *Shared Traditions: Southern History and Folk Culture*. Champaign: University of Illinois Press.

Kabbani, Rana (1994) *Imperial Fictions: Europe's Myths of Orient*. London: Pandora Press.

Kamps, Ivo and Jysotsna G. Singh (eds) (2001) *Travel Knowledge: European 'Discoveries' in the Early Modern Period*. London: Palgrave.

Kamps, Ivo and Jysotsna G. Singh (2001) 'Introduction.' In Ivo Kamps and Jysotsna G. Singh (eds), *Travel Knowledge: European 'Discoveries' in the Early Modern Period*. London: Palgrave, pp. 1–16.

Karp, Jonathan and Adam Sutcliffe (eds) (2011) *Philosemitism in History*. Cambridge: Cambridge University Press.

Kidd, Thomas S. (2003). '"Is it worse to follow Mahomet than the Devil?": Early American Uses of Islam.' *Church History*, 72: 766–790.

Klein, Deitrich and Birte Platow (eds) (2008) *Wahrnehmung des Islam zwischen Reformation und Aufklärung*. München: Wilhelm Fink.

Konrad, Felix (2011) 'From the "Turkish Menace" to Exoticism and Orientalism: Islam as Antithesis of Europe (1453–1914)?' in *European History Online* (EGO), URL: http://www.ieg-ego.eu/konradf-2010-en (accessed 12 December 2012).

Korshin, Paul J. (1984) 'Queuing and Waiting: The Apocalypse in England, 1660–1715.' In C. A. Patrides and Joseph Wittreich (eds), *The Apocalypse in English Renaissance Thought and Literature: Patterns, Antecedents and Repercussions*. Manchester: Manchester University Press, pp. 240–265.

Krstić, Tijana (2011) *Contested Conversions to Islam: Narratives of Religious Change in the Early Modern Ottoman Empire*. Palo Alto: Stanford University Press.

Kuran-Burçoğlu, Nedret (2005). *Die Wandlung des Türkenbildes in Europa: Vom 11. Jahrhundert bis zur heutigen Zeit; Eine kritische Perspektive*. Zürich: Spur.

Lambert, Frank (2005) *The Barbary Wars: American Independence in the Atlantic World*. New York: Hill and Wang.

Lerner, Robert E. (1983) *The Powers of Prophecy: The Cedar of Lebanon Vision from the Mongol Onslaught to the Dawn of the Enlightenment*. Berkeley: University of California Press.

Lewis, Bernard (1982) *The Muslim Discovery of Europe*. New York: W. W. Norton.

Lewis, Bernard (1993) 'Corsairs in Iceland.' In *Islam in History: Ideas, People and Events in the Middle East*. Chicago: Open Court, pp. 239–245.

Lisboa, Maria Manuel (2011) *The End of the World: Apocalypse and Its Aftermath in Western Culture*. Cambridge: Open Book Publishers.

Loomba, Ania (2002) *Shakespeare, Race, and Colonialism*. Oxford: Oxford University Press.

Lovejoy, Paul E. (1989) 'The Impact of the Atlantic Slave Trade on Africa: A Review of the Literature.' *Journal of African History*, 30: 365–394.

Lyons, William John and Jorunn Økland (eds) (2009) *The Way the World Ends?: The Apocalypse of John in Culture and Ideology*. Sheffield: Sheffield Phoenix Press.

Mack, Phyllis (1992) *Visionary Women: Ecstatic Prophecy in Seventeenth-Century England*. Berkeley: University of California Press.

MacLean, Gerald (2007) *Looking East: English Writing and the Ottoman Empire Before 1800*. London: Palgrave Macmillan.

MacLean, Gerald and Nabil Matar (2011) *Britain and the Islamic World*. Oxford: Oxford University Press.

Marr, Timothy (2006) *The Cultural Roots of American Islamicism*. Cambridge: Cambridge University Press.

Matar, Nabil (1989) 'Some Notes on George Fox and Islam.' *Journal of the Friends' Historical Society*, 55: 271–276.

Matar, Nabil (1993) 'The Renegade in English Seventeenth-Century Imagination.' *Studies in English Literature 1500–1900*, 33.3: 489–505.

Matar, Nabil (1997) 'Muslims in Seventeenth-Century England.' *Journal of Islamic Studies*, 8: 63–82.

Matar, Nabil. (1998a) *Islam in Britain 1558–1685*. Cambridge: Cambridge University Press.

Matar, Nabil (1998b) 'Alexander Ross and the first English translation of the Qur'an.' *The Muslim World*, 88.1: 81–92.

Matar, Nabil (1999) *Turks, Moors, and Englishmen in the Age of Discovery*. New York: Columbia University Press.

Matar, Nabil (2001a) 'The Barbary Corsairs, King Charles I and the Civil War.' *The Seventeenth Century*, 16.2: 239–258.

Matar, Nabil (2001b) 'Introduction: England and Mediterranean Captivity 1577–1704.' In Daniel Vitkus (ed.), *Piracy, Slavery and Redemption: Barbary Captivity Narratives from Early Modern England*. New York: Columbia University Press, pp. 1–52.

Matar, Nabil (2003) *In the Lands of the Christians: Arabic Travel Writing in the Seventeenth Century*. London: Routledge.

Matar, Nabil (2005a) *Britain and Barbary: 1589–1689*. Gainesville: University Press of Florida.

Matar, Nabil (2005b) 'Anglo-Muslim Disputation in the Early Modern Period.' In Matthew Birchwood and Matthew Dimmock (eds), *Cultural Encounters Between East and West, 1453–1699*. Newcastle: Cambridge Scholars Press, pp. 29–42.

Matthee, Rudi (2009) 'The Safavids under Western Eyes: Seventeenth-Century European Travelers to Iran.' *Journal of Early Modern History*, 13.2: 137–171.

Mather, James (2009) *Pashas: Traders and Travellers in the Islamic World*. New Haven: Yale University Press.

McGinn, Bernard (1994) *Antichrist: Two Thousand Years of the Human Fascination with Evil*. San Francisco: Harper Collins.

McGinn, Bernard (1998) *Visions of the End: Apocalyptic Traditions in the Middle Ages*. Second edition. New York: Columbia University Press.

Meggitt, Justin J. (2011) 'Naked Quakers: Apocalyptic Obsessions and Public Nudity – the World of the Early Quakers.' *Fortean Times*, 271: 38–42.

Menocal, María Rosa (2002) *The Ornament of the World: How Muslims, Jews, and Christians Created a Culture of Tolerance in Medieval Spain*. Boston: Little, Brown and Co.

Menocal, María Rosa, Raymond P. Scheindlin, and Michael Sells (eds) (2000) *The Cambridge History of Arabic Literature: The Literature of al-Andalus*. Cambridge: Cambridge University Press.

Meyerson, Mark D. (1996) 'Slavery and Solidarity: Mudejars and Foreign Muslim Captives in the Kingdom of Valencia'. *Medieval Encounters*, 2.3: 286–343.

Miller, John (2005) '"A Suffering People": English Quakers and Their Neighbours c.1650–c.1700.' *Past & Present*, 188: 71–103.

Miller, Kathryn A. (2008) *Guardians of Islam: Religious Authority and Muslim Communities of Late Medieval Spain*. New York: Columbia University Press.

Mills, Simon (2011) 'The English Chaplains at Aleppo: Exploration and Scholarship Between England and the Ottoman Empire, 1620–1760.' *Bulletin of the Council for British Research in the Levant*, 6.1: 13–20.

Moore, Rosemary E. (2000) *The Light in their Consciences: Early Quakers in Britain 1646–1666*. University Park: Penn State University Press.

Mortimer, Russell (ed.) (1971) *Minute Book of the Men's Meeting of the Society of Friends in Bristol 1667–1686*. Bristol: Bristol Record Society.

Morton, A. L. (1966) *The Everlasting Gospel: A Study in the Sources of William Blake*. New York: Haskell House.

Myers, Albert C. (ed.) (1912) *Narratives of Early Pennsylvania, West New Jersey and Delaware, 1630–1707*. New York: Charles Scribner's Sons.

Nadalo, Stephanie (2011) 'Negotiating Slavery in a Tolerant Frontier: Livorno's Turkish Bagno (1547–1747).' *Mediaevalia*, 32: 275–324.

New England Historic Genealogical Society (1984) *English Origins of New England Families: From the New England Historical and Genealogical Register, First Series*. Volume 3. Baltimore: Genealogical Publishing Company.

Page, Nicholas (2001) *Lord Minimus: The Extraordinary Life of Britain's Smallest Man*. London: HarperCollins.

Parker, Kenneth (ed.) (1999) *Early Modern Tales of Orient: A Critical Anthology*. London: Routledge.

Parrinder, Geoffrey (2002) *Jesus in the Qur'an*. Oxford: Oneworld.

Penney, Norman (ed.) (1907) *'The first publishers of truth': being early records (now first printed) of the introduction of Quakerism into the counties of England and Wales*. London: Headley brothers.

Peters, K. (2005) *Print Culture and the Early Quakers*. Cambridge: Cambridge University Press.

Pickvance, T. J. (1989) *A Reader's Companion to George Fox's Journal*. London: Quaker Home Service.

Popkin, Richard H. (1985) 'Spinoza and Samuel Fisher.' *Philosophia*, 15: 219–236.

Popkin, R. and J. Force (eds) (2001) *The Millenarian Turn: Millenarian Contexts of Science, Politics, and Everyday Anglo-American Life in the Seventeenth and Eighteenth Centuries; Millenarianism and Messianism in Early Modern European Culture*: Volume III. Dordrecht: Kluwer.

Porter, Dennis (1993) 'Oreintalism and its Problems', in Patrick Williams and Laura Chrisman (eds), *Colonial discourse and post-colonial theory: a reader*. Hemel Hempstead: Harvester Wheatsheaf, pp. 150–161.

Pratt, Mary Louise (1986) 'Fieldwork in Common Places.' In James Clifford and George E. Marcus (eds), *Writing Culture: The Poetics and Politics of Ethnography*. London: University of California Press, pp. 27–50.

Rawlins, Sophia W. (1951) 'Joseph and Alexander Harbin: Two Barbadian Merchants, Their Families and Descendants.' *Journal of the Barbados Museum Historical Society*, 19: 28–33.

Reay, Barry (1985) *The Quakers and the English Revolution*. London: Temple Smith.

Reeves, Minou (2003) *Muhammad in Europe: A Thousand Years of Western Myth-Making*. New York: NYU Press.

Richardson, R. C. (1998) *The Debate on the English Revolution*. Third edition: Manchester University Press.

Riddell, William Renwick (1930) 'A Half-Told Story of Real White Slavery in the Seventeenth Century.' *Journal of the American Institute of Criminal Law and Criminology*, 21.2: 247–253.

Rodinson, Maxime (2002) *Europe and the Mystique of Islam*. London: I. B. Tauris.

Russell, G. A. (1994) *The 'Arabick' Interest of the Natural Philosophers in Seventeenth-Century England*. Leiden: Brill.

Ryan, James Emmett (2009) *Imaginary Friends: Representing Quakers in American Culture 1650–1950*. Wisconsin: University of Wisconsin Press.

Said, Edward W. (1980) *L'orientalisme: l'Orient créé par l'Occident*. Paris: Seuil.

Said, Edward W. (1997 [1981]) *Covering Islam*. Second edition. London: Vintage.

Said, Edward W. (2003 [1978]) *Orientalism*. Third edition. London: Penguin.

Sapra, Rahul (2011) *The Limits of Orientalism: Seventeenth-Century Representations of India*. Newark: University of Delaware Press.

Schen, Claire S. (2000) 'Constructing the Poor in Early Seventeenth-Century London.' *Albion: A Quarterly Journal Concerned with British Studies*, 32: 450–463.

Scholem, Gershom G. (1976) *Sabbatai Sevi: The Mystical Messiah, 1626–1676*. Second edition. Princeton: Princeton University Press.

Sheppard, Walter Lee (1992) *Passengers and Ships Prior to 1684*. Philadelphia: Welcome Society of Pennsylvania.

Schwarz, Suzanne (2008) *Slave Captain: The Career of James Irving in the Liverpool Slave trade*. Second edition. Liverpool: Liverpool University Press.

Setton, Kenneth Meyer (1991) *Venice, Austria, and the Turks in the Seventeenth Century*. Philadelphia: The American Philosophical Society.

Setton, Kenneth Meyer (1992) *Western Hostility to Islam and Prophecies of Turkish Doom*. Philadelphia: American Philosophical Society.

Sha'ban, Faud (1991). *Islam and Arabs in Early American Thought: Roots of Orientalism in America*. Durham: Acorn Press.

Sha'ban, Fuad (2005) *For Zion's Sake: The Judeao-Christian Tradition in American Culture*. London: Pluto Press, 2005.

Smith, Joseph (1873) *Bibliotheca anti-Quakeriana*. London: Joseph Smith.

Snader, Joe (2000) *Caught Between Worlds: British Captivity Narratives in Fact and Fiction*. Lexington: University Press of Kentucky.

Southern, R. W. (1962) *Western Views of Islam in the Middle Ages*. Cambridge MA: Harvard University Press.

Spencer, C. (2007) *Holiness: The Soul of Quakerism*. Milton Keynes: Paternoster Press.

Starr, G. A. (1965) 'Escape from Barbary: A Seventeenth-Century Genre.' *Huntington Library Quarterly*, 29: 35–52.

Steenbrink, Karel A. (2006) *Dutch Colonialism and Indonesian Islam: Contacts and Conflicts, 1596–1950*. Second edition. New York: Editions Rodopi B.V.

Thomas, Kathleen (1996) 'An Evaluation of the Doctrine of the Inward Light as a Basis for Mission as Exemplified by Quaker Approaches to Jews and Muslims.' *Quaker Studies*, 1: 54–72.

Thomas, Keith (1958) 'Women and the Civil War Sects.' *Past & Present*, 13.1: 42–63.

Thompson, Janice E. (1994) *Mercenaries, Pirates, and Sovereigns: State-Building and Extra-Territorial Violence in Early Modern Europe*. Princeton: Princeton University Press.

Tinniswood, Adrian (2010) *Pirates of Barbary: Corsairs, Conquests and Captivity in the 17th-Century Mediterranean*. London: Jonathan Cape.

Tolan, John Victor (2002) *Saracens: Islam in the Medieval European Imagination*. New York: Columbia University Press.

Tolan, John, Henry Laurens, and Gilles Vernstein (2012) *Saracens: Europe and the Islamic World: A History*. Princetown: Princetown University Press.

Tolles, Fredrick B. (1963a) 'Nonviolent Contact: The Quakers and the Indians.' *Proceedings of the American Philosophical Society*, 107.2: 93–101.

Tolles, Fredrick B. (1963b) *Meeting House and Counting House*. New York: W. W. Norton.

Toon, Peter (1970) *Puritans, the Millennium and the Future of Israel: Puritan Eschatology 1600–1660*. Cambridge: James Clarke & Co.

Tuke, Samuel (1848) *Account of the Slavery of Friends in the Barbary States*. London: Marsh.

Turley, Hans (1999) *Rum, Sodomy, and the Lash: Piracy, Sexuality, and Masculine Identity*. New York: NYU Press.

Underwood, T. L. (1997) *Primitivism, Radicalism, and the Lamb's War: The Baptist-Quaker Conflict in Seventeenth-Century England*. Oxford: Oxford University Press.

Van Der Beets, Richard (1994) *Held captive by Indians: Selected Narratives, 1642–1836*. Second edition. Knoxville: University of Tennessee Press.

Van Koningsveld, P. S. (1995) 'Muslim Slaves and Captives in Western Europe During the Late Middle Ages.' *Islam and Christian–Muslim Relations*, 6.1: 5–23.

Vaughan, Alden T. (1986) *Puritans Among the Indians: Accounts of Captivity and Redemption, 1676–1724*. Cambridge MA: Harvard University Press.

Villani, Stefano (1996) *Tremolanti e Papisti: missioni quacchere nell'Italia del seicento*. Rome: Edizioni di Storia e Letteratura.

Villani, Stefano (1998) 'I quaccheri contro il Papa: Alcuni pamphlet inglesi del '600 tra menzogne e verità.' *Studi Secenteschi*, 38: 165–202.

Villani, Stefano (2001) *Il Calzolaio Quacchero e Il Finto Cadì*. Palermo: Sellerio.

Villani, Stefano (ed.) (2003) *A True Account of the Great Tryals and Cruel Sufferings Undergone by Those Two Faithful Servants of God Katherine Evans and Sarah Cheevers, London 1663. La vicenda di due quacchere prigioniere dell'inquisizione di Malta. Scuola Normale Superiore*. Pisa: Scuola Normale Superiore.

Villani, Stefano (2004) 'Fisher, Mary (c.1623–1698).' *Oxford Dictionary of National Biography*. Volume 19. Oxford: Oxford University Press, pp. 706–707.

Vitkus, Daniel (1999) 'Early Modern Orientalism: Representations of Islam in Sixteenth and Seventeenth-Century Europe.' In D. Blanks and M. Frassetto (eds), *Western Views of Islam in edieval and Early Modern Europe*. New York: St. Martin's Press, pp. 207–230.

Vitkus, Daniel (2000) 'Trafficking with the Turk: English Travelers in the Ottoman Empire during the Seventeenth Century.' In Jyotsna G. Singh and Ivo Kamps (eds), *Travel Knowledge: European Witnesses to 'Navigations, Traffiques, and Discoveries' in the Early Modern Period*. New York: St. Martin's Press, pp. 35–52.

Vitkus, Daniel (2001) *Piracy, Slavery, and Redemption: Barbary Captivity Narratives from Early Modern England*. New York: Columbia University Press.

Vlasblom, David (2011) 'Islam in Early Modern Quaker Experience and Writing.' *Quaker History*, 100.1: 1–21.

Watt, Willam M. (1991) *Muslim-Christian Encounters: Perceptions and Misperceptions.* London: Routledge.

Waysblum, M. (1959) 'A Quaker in Barbary: Thomas Hutson in Algiers.' *Journal of the Friends' Historical Society,* 49: 109–111.

Webster, Jeremy W. (2006) 'The "Lustful Buggering Jew": Anti-Semitism, Gender, and Sodomy in Restoration Political Satire.' *Journal for Early Modern Cultural Studies,* 6.1: 106–124.

Weddle, Meredith Baldwin (2001) *Walking in the Way of Peace: Quaker Pacifism in the Seventeenth Century.* New York: Oxford University Press.

Weiss, Gillian (2011) *Captives and Corsairs: France and Slavery in the Early Modern Mediterranean.* Stanford: Stanford University Press.

Wiegers, Gerard (1992) 'A Life between Europe and the Maghrib: the writings and travels of Ahmad b. Qâsim al-Hajarî al-Andalusî (born ca. 977/1569–70).' In Geert Jan van Gelder and E. de Moor (eds), *The Middle East and Europe: Encounters and Exchanges.* Amsterdam: Rodopi, pp. 87–115.

Wiggins, Rosalind Cobb (ed.) *Captain Paul Cuffe's Logs and Letters, 1808–1817: A Black Quaker's 'Voice from Within the Veil'.* Washington: Howard University Press.

Williams, George Hunston (1992) *The Radical Reformation.* Third edition. Kirkville: Sixteenth Century Essays & Studies.

Williamson, Arthur H. (2008) *Apocalypse Then: Prophecy and the Making of the Modern World.* Westport: Praeger.

Woolrych, A. (2002) *Britain in Revolution: 1625–1660.* Oxford: Oxford University Press.

Wright, Melanie J. (2009) '"Every Eye Shall See Him": Revelation and Film.' In William John Lyons and Jorunn Økland (eds), *The Way the World Ends?: The Apocalypse of John in Culture and Ideology.* Sheffield: Sheffield Phoenix Press, pp. 76–94.

STUDIES ON INTER-RELIGIOUS RELATIONS
STUDIER AV INTER-RELIGIÖSA RELATIONER

Editors/utgivare: Ingvar Svanberg & David Westerlund

17. Greg Simons, *The Russian Orthodox Church and its role in cultural production.* Stockholm: Almqvist & Wiksell International, 2005.
18. Terje Østebø, *A history of Islam and inter-religious relations in Bale, Ethiopia.* Stockholm: Almqvist & Wiksell International, 2005.
19. Christer Hedin, *Tor Andrae och orientalismen.* Uppsala: Swedish Science Press, 2005.
20. Hege Irene Markussen & Richard Johan Natvig (red.), *Islamer i Norge.* Uppsala: Swedish Science Press, 2005.
21. Håkan Rydving (red.), *Religion og nasjon: fire studier.* Uppsala. Swedish Science Press, 2005.
22. Mohammad Fazlhashemi, *Occidentalism: idéer om väst och modernitet bland muslimska tänkare.* Lund: Studentlitteratur, 2005.
23. On Barak, *Names without faces: from polemics to flirtation in Islamic chat-room nicknaming.* Stockholm: Almqvist & Wiksell International, 2006.
24. Lars Dencik, *Judendom i Sverige: en sociologisk belysning.* Uppsala: Swedish Science Press, 2006.
25. Susanne Olsson, *Islam and the West in the ideology of Hasan Hanafi.* Stockholm: Almqvist & Wiksell International, 2006.
26. Christer Hedin, *Ali Shariatis befrielseteologi: västerländska inslag i shiitisk revolutionär islam.* Uppsala: Swedish Science Press, 2006.
27. David Westerlund (red.), *Vodou, santeria, olivorism: om afro-amerikanska religioner.* Göteborg & Stockholm: Makadam, 2006.
28. Tina Hamrin-Dahl, *Aleviter i Turkiet.* Uppsala: Swedish Science Press, 2006.
29. Göran Larsson (ed.), *Religious communities on the Internet: proceedings from a conference.* Uppsala: Swedish Science Press, 2006.
30. Galina Lindquist, *The quest for the authentic shaman: multiple meanings of shamanism on a Siberian journey.* Stockholm: Almqvist & Wiksell International, 2006.
31. Muhammed Haron, *The dynamics of Christian-Muslim relations in South Africa (ca 1960–2000): from exclusivism to pluralism.* Stockholm: Almqvist & Wiksell International, 2006.
32. Göran Larsson, *Muslimerna kommer! Tankar om islamofobi.* Göteborg & Stockholm: Makadam, 2006.
33. Ruth Illman, *Ett annorlunda Du: reflektioner kring religionsdialog.* Göteborg & Stockholm: Makadam, 2006.
34. Simon Stjernholm, *The struggle for purity: Naqshbandi-Haqqani Sufism in London.* Uppsala: Swedish Science Press, 2006.
35. Helena Norman, *Religion som medieberättelse: Expressens rapportering om Knutbyfallet.* Uppsala: Swedish Science Press, 2007.
36. Sidsel Lied, *Kristne friskoler i en flerkulturell kontekst.* Uppsala: Swedish Science Press & Vallset: Oplandske bokförlag, 2007.

37. Garbi Schmidt, *Muslim i Danmark – muslim i verden: en analyse af muslimske ungdomsforeninger og muslimsk identitet i årene op til Muhammad-krisen.* København: SFI – Det Nationale Forsk-ningscenter for Valfærd & Uppsala: Swedish Science Press, 2007.

38. Philip Halldén, *Jihad-orienterad salafism på internet.* Uppsala: Swedish Science Press, 2007.

39. E. G. Kanikova, *Muslims in Bulgaria.* Uppsala: Swedish Science Press, 2007.

40. Olle Sundström, *Kampen mot "schamanismen": sovjetisk religionspolitik gentemot inhemska religioner i Sibirien och norra Ryssland.* Uppsala: Swedish Science Press, 2007.

41. Tabona Shoko, *Spiritual healing in Zimbabwe: continuity and change.* Uppsala: Swedish Science Press, 2008.

42. Willy Pfändtner & David Thurfjell (eds), *Postcolonial challenges to the study of religion.* Uppsala: Swedish Science Press, 2008.

43. Lena Roos & Jenny Berglund (eds), *Your heritage and mine: teaching in a multi-religious classroom.* Uppsala: Swedish Science Press, 2009.

44. Göran Larsson (ed.), *Islam in the Nordic and Baltic countries.* London & New York: Routledge, 2009.

45. David Westerlund (ed.), *Global Pentecostalism: encounters with other religious traditions.* London & New York: I.B. Tauris, 2009.

46. David Westerlund, *Islam eller kristendom? Nutida polemik och konflikter mellan kristna och muslimer.* Stockholm: Dialogos, 2009.

47. Lovemore Togarasei & Ezra Chitando (eds), *Faith in the city: the role and place of religion in Harare.* Uppsala: Swedish Science Press, 2010.

48. Thomas McElwain, *Adventism and Ellen White: a phenomenon of religious materialism.* Uppsala: Swedish Science Press, 2010.

49. Kristian Steiner, *"Vem är min nästa?" Bilden av islam och muslimer i den kristna nyhetstidningen Världen idag.* Uppsala: Swedish Science Press, 2010.

50. Karl G. Jechoutek, *The diversity ethic and the spirit of individualism: religious and economic strategies in hybrid Cape Town.* Uppsala: Swedish Science Press, 2011.

51. Hans Olsson, *The politics of interfaith institutions in contemporary Tanzania.* Uppsala: Swedish Science Press, 2011.

52. Thomas Bossius, Andreas Häger & Keith Kahn-Harris (eds), *Religion and popular music in Europe: new expressions of sacred and secular identity.* London & New York: I.B. Tauris, 2011.

53. Göran Larsson & Susanne Olsson (red.), *Islam och politik.* Lund: Studentlitteratur, 2011.

54. Elena Namli & Ingvar Svanberg, *Religion och politik i Ryssland.* Uppsala: Swedish Science Press, 2012.

55. Mikael Stenmark, *Religioner i konflikt: relationen mellan kristen och muslimsk tro.* Stockholm: Dialogos, 2012.

56. Anne-Christine Hornborg, *Coaching och lekmannaterapi: en modern väckelse?* Stockholm: Dialogos, 2012.
57. David Thurfjell, *Faith and revivalism in a Nordic Romani community: Pentecostalism amongst the Kaale Roma of Sweden and Finland.* London & New York: I.B. Tauris, 2013.
58. Susanne Olsson (red.), *Sällskapet: tro och vetande i 1900-talets Sverige.* Stockholm: Molin & Sorgenfrei, 2013.
59. Justin J. Meggitt, *Early Quakers and Islam: Slavery, Apocalyptic and Christian-Muslim Encounters in the Seventeenth Century.* Uppsala: Swedish Science Press, 2013.

www.ingramcontent.com/pod-product-compliance
Lightning Source LLC
Chambersburg PA
CBHW060418090426

42734CB00011B/2352